DESPERATE HOUSEPETS

The Single Person's Guide to Healthy Pets

Annaliese Morgan

Illustrated by Kate Crowther

IndePenPress

First published in Great Britain by Indepenpress
All paper used in the printing of this book has been made from wood grown in
managed, sustainable forests.

ISBN13: 978-1-78003-145-3

Indepenpress Publishers Ltd
25 Eastern Place
Brighton
BN2 1GJ

Printed and bound in the UK

A catalogue record of this book is available from
the British Library

Cover design and illustrations by Kate Crowther

Acknowledgements

The following people are those rock solid people that I am lucky to have in my life. You all deserve massive thanks and mean far more than I can say. Mwah xx

My moogle bears, Max and Woody – your love, care, humour, hugs and kisses make me understand what it's all about and I love you both.

Mum and Tom –You have knowledge and wisdom I can only hope to achieve half of. You both keep me upright on so many levels. We are forever the ring of steel.

The Woodheads – There isn't many of us but boy are we all made of top stuff!

Carol and Benji, Mark and Rebecca Hoogland, Mark and Laura Kitchen, Emma Howarth BVMS (Hons) MRCVS, Rosanna and her Creative Beauty (not forgetting Rupert and of course Mr Coco Cream Chanel!), Eddie – So many years, so many memories, none of which I would trade. Thank you for your amazing friendships.

Ian Court - I know you always look forward to my rambling emails! Honestly though, you've kept things possible.

Amy Bottomley and Charlotte Orme – I learn from you two every day and proud to have you as my team, Me and Coolio will C U When U Get There!

Kate – Thank you for being an absolute pleasure to work with and for the time you always put into my craziness!

With huge thanks for their past and current support – National Veterinary Services, Royal Canin, Virbac Animal Health UK, Bayer, Merial, CEVA Animal Health. All the fabulous pets and their wonderful owners at Fuchsia.

Annaliese

From Kate:

I would like to thank the following beautiful sources of inspiration for all the drawings:

Lulu for her lovely teeth and ears, Murphy for being a cute pup, Rolo the gentle giant and Coco, the not so mean in real life Chihuahua, Eric the cat, Michael the Beagle and last but definitely not least, Digby. The best dog in the world and the reason I started drawing again.

I would also like to thank Annaliese for letting me do this project, amazing what can come from going out of your comfort zone.

Previous publications:

How to get through NVQ 2 for Veterinary Nurses

How to get through NVQ 3 for Veterinary Nurses

A – Z for Veterinary Nurses

'Ananesthesia and Analgesia'
chapter in the *BSAVA Manual of Veterinary Nursing*

Preface

I speak to pet owners every day and it still surprises me how much confusion and a genuine lack of understanding there is. Oh and the myths, so many myths, these are bandied about year after year and to be honest are usually not worth listening to. Something else that doesn't help is that there are those who are more than happy to listen to so-and-so down the road, the woman in the chip shop, or their best friend's cousin's aunty rather than seek or believe the advice from professionals. For your pet's sake, always find the best advice you can, be it from vets, veterinary nurses or other trained professionals. We are all here to look after your pets, that's why we trained in the first place and why we still do our jobs today. There are as well, just as many owners (if not more), who try to understand everything they can about their pet and will follow all the guidelines or ask if they are unsure. Although there are types at either end of the scale and many in between, most have one thing in common – they love their pet and will do anything for them.

I've spent so many years in the veterinary profession (18 so far) and absolutely love it. I have spent some incredible years in practice and worked with some truly amazing people (and some horrors!). Although I do miss being in practice and my old colleagues, the point came where I wanted my own business. I wanted to be the big wheel, rather than the cog in someone else's big wheel. I wanted to do things my way, care for the pets and their owners how I felt they should be and to take how we look after our pets to a unique level.

Originating in July 2008, (with sheer hard work and determination) I opened 'Fuchsia', a pet health spa and boutique. Bringing together a unique pet experience, aspiring to keep pets happy, healthy and beautiful. In a luxury environment, my team and I dedicate a huge amount of time, care and support, to ensure we achieve this. An understanding of pets' wants and needs, can make such a difference to them, to you and your family. Even the reasons behind simple requirements are important and should be recognised. Hopefully the owners I work with now feel they can come and ask me anything, no matter how small or big they think it may be. Listening is one of the most important tools to be gifted with and I will only work with people who use this tool, along with passion and their professional qualifications. Our fashonista pets and owners are, therefore, always provided with genuine advice and care.

This guide to pet care follows on from that – I wanted to give you, the pet owners, a trendy but realistic guide to healthy pets but most importantly, why, without boring you to tears. Hopefully, all those who read this will find it informative, interesting and entertaining, yet feel the genuine passion that I do.

And finally, from me personally: 'They say' that difficult and tough situations which, undoubtedly cross our lives, strengthen our character and values. Although I have wondered over the years just how much strengthening I needed and was it all really necessary? The answer is probably yes. Is my drive for life, my career, to juggle home life, being mummy and yummy due to all the previous difficult times I've endured? Or, is it due to amazing parents, the doctors who kept me alive and eventually, got me out of a wheelchair and walking again? Or is it down to people who didn't care or believe in me, or people I love and look up to? Who knows, but maybe each one of them deserves a big thank you for making me the person I am today.

Annaliese Morgan
Dip AVN(Surgical) RVN MBVNA

This book is dedicated to

Tim

My one and only brother
Gone too soon and missed everyday

May 1977 – May 2007

xxx

About the Author

I began carving out my career in veterinary nursing in 1993, qualifying in 1997. I went on to gain assessor qualifications in 2000 enabling me to train other veterinary nurses within practice. In 2002 I obtained the Advanced Veterinary Nursing Surgical Diploma (currently there are about 250 nurses in the UK that hold this qualification). I spent 15 adorable years in small animal and mixed veterinary practice, the last 10 of those in senior positions running the nursing departments and many aspects of veterinary practice. I passed a further exam enabling me to prescribe and dispense certain pet medications in my own right and opened my very own unique pet health spa called Fuchsia in July 2008. In October 2008 I was honoured to receive the VN Times Award by The British Veterinary Nursing Association for my continued work within veterinary nursing.

My love of writing and my first published book evolved in 2004; to be now on my 5th book, whilst running my own wonderful business 'Fuchsia', I find quite unreal and incredibly rewarding. Never underestimate passion!

I live in a tiny village amongst the hills in Huddersfield with my two boys, two ancient cats and Michael the Beagle! Loving my life, with all that it does and may bring.

Contents

I want one of those!

So you've made your decision you're going to get a pet – or it could be your little angels have worn you down about getting the best thing you ever could for them and you can't bear another tear-stained letter, or Oscar night winning performance asking for a dog. There are though, many things to consider before making your choice, even if you are an experienced pet owner.

Whether you are single, a professional couple, lady of the manor or a member of a family the same rule applies – the pet you choose must fit into your environment and lifestyle. For example, if you live in a trendy apartment (even if it is the penthouse) a Great Dane is not a great idea. If though, you have a fair amount of time and would like a loving family pet, then something like a Bichon Frise is perfect. Although discussing the requirements of different pets and breeds is beyond the scope of this book (there are others for this), I want to mention areas that need consideration **before** deciding on your latest addition:

Are You Sure You Have the Time

Perhaps one of the most important points to consider, how much time do you realistically have? And how much of that time are you realistically going to dedicate to your pet? Work, feeding, walking, grooming, vet trips, holidays, children's hobbies and play time all need to be factored in. Will you honestly get up an hour earlier to walk the dog, appealing in the summer but what about the winter months when it's cold and dark and you are all warm and cosy under your duvet, with the central heating on?

We all set out with the best intentions, but don't let walkies turn in to a run around your garden, for both your pet's sake and your enjoyment. By the same token, some dogs I know are over-excised. Old dogs with arthritis for example do not need a two-hour walk (short and often for these ones, please). Little dogs like Chihuahuas are unlikely to want to go hiking on the moors; a Beagle on the other hand could out run most athletes! Don't get me wrong there are always the exceptions. Although walking your dog has to be done, it also provides lots of positives – exercise for you, family time (take the children, bikes, even your partner!). I use it for 'me time' – iPod gets plugged in and off I go – love it! Just be sure to place your dog's exercise and training needs with what you **can and will** do, therefore you are more likely to gain the enjoyment and fun of owning a pet. If you don't have the time to provide the walks and exercise your particular dog needs, boredom, amongst other problems is going to set in. Trouble is, a bored dog will often chew (personally if I'm bored I like to shop!) but many people complain their dog 'chews everything'.

Remember this is down to you, choice of dog, training, environment for example and not the dog deliberately trying to wind you up – although, if they have a gone through your new pair of Manolos, I can understand a few choice words!

Day Care, it's Not Just For the Children!

You can of course use dog walkers and doggy day care (I use this for a couple of days a week and Michael the Beagle absolutely loves it). Take care when choosing as there are now a lot of these about and, to be frank, you want to stay away from the ones who think it's an easy way of making a few extra quid. We only like the real deal!

The National Association of Registered Pet Sitters or National Missing Pets Register (see Useful Contacts) are good sources of information.

Remember to check their insurance, who pays for what should your dog injure themselves or someone else whilst in their care?

Don't forget common sense questions such as, where do they get walked, how long for, can they medicate your pet if required. Any reputable sitter or day care should also insist on vaccinations just as boarding kennels/catteries do.

Whilst our pooches love to go out and work the scene, cats are far too important to do that and much prefer to stay in their own environments and have staff come to them! Services for cats are therefore on the increase. They will come to your house and feed your cat, some provide extras such as playing, changing the litter tray, grooming, and most are offering holiday cover, so you don't have to put your cat into a cattery whilst you are away. Keep your sensible head on when choosing people to help, as you are giving them access to your home.

Cats and their Mysterious Ways

Cats are much more independent and demand less of your time – many are quite happy as long as they are fed, warm and can go in and out as they please, yes, someone else who uses the house as a hotel! However they don't come without their own considerations – will they be indoor only cats or will they go out? Indoor cats need lots more environmental enrichments, toys, hiding places, scratching facilities for example. Do you live near a busy road? Do you have the time to spend on grooming? Will you want them to use a litter tray or go outside?

Speaking of litter trays, oh how these can cause hassle and take up so much of our precious time while we clean everything up (unless the dog has emptied it for you that is, by eating the contents!). We all know the smell can become pretty potent, so whilst you may not want the tray in your sitting room (as you can guarantee they will produce the worst smelling poo whilst you have guests over!), careful consideration is needed with litter trays, or your cat just won't use it.

Getting the tray situation wrong means more often than not, they will decide for themselves where they want to go, which is usually where you don't. They need placing in the correct areas, not in front of windows, French doors or areas where the local feline posse can view them. The number of trays is also significant as is the type of litter. The usually rule here is, have one more tray than you have cats and don't seat them next to each other, have them in different areas. It appears cats have their own Feng Shui with their belongings! Stress causes a lot of problems in cats, inappropriate weeing is one of them. I remember an occasion where I thought I had a leaking pipe in the bathroom and after calling out the plumber, everyone was scratching their heads as to what it was. It turned out to be my old cat objecting to the recent house move! Yes, I did feel stupid!

Cat behaviour is so worth looking into – fascinating.

How Much?!

If you are purchasing a pedigree cat or dog you are almost certain to pay a few hundred pounds; you can of course adopt a rescue pet, sometimes free of charge or sometimes with minimal charges to aid the charities that do this (see Useful Contacts).

With regard to on-going costs the usual feeding, vet and health treatments, grooming and even accessories like collars there is a simple rule here; the bigger they are the more they are going to cost. The costs rise with size – the bigger the pets the more they will eat, vet bills will be higher (they will need higher doses of medications for example) and grooming will take longer. I know, I know, I'm pointing out the obvious, but again some miss this completely, then blame the vet, the groomer, the pet shop or the man in Surrey making the pet food, for how much they are being charged and ripped off. If you haven't already guessed, this personally annoys me, THINK ON before you get your pet, check prices of vets, groomers, foods etc. etc. so you know what to expect and can budget accordingly.

Vet bills can be extremely expensive so please, if you only remember one thing make sure it's insurance, insurance, insurance, unfortunately there is no NHS for pets. So many times owners are placed in heartbreaking and difficult predicaments because they can't afford the treatment (it guts us as well).

Although pet insurance will not pay for preventative care such as vaccinations, it will remove the worry of how to pay the vet's bill should they become ill or have an accident. Remember the older they get the more aliments they will have as well, a lot of which are covered by pet insurance. Therefore, you can concentrate on getting your pet better and maintaining their quality of life. There are many companies offering pet insurance, the cheapest one may not always be the better option. Check the small print, do they offer to pay for the life of the illness or just a set amount of time or money? Are there certain conditions, foods, treatments they won't cover? Any veterinary practice offering pet insurance will have a member of staff who is an 'appointed insurance representative' (I'm the appointed insurance representative for Fuchsia). These representatives have undergone extra training and are a requirement in today's web of insurance rules and regulations. They are the only ones able to discuss queries, different polices and offer advice where needed. It is worth asking about the practice's policy for payment – do they expect you to pay the full amount of the bill and the insurance company to reimburse you, or do they bill the insurance company directly? As with any insurance there is always an excess to pay, so please take this into consideration.

I'll share a story here. An old man who I'll call George had been a client for years; he and his wife had taken on a cat which had a survived a severe cruelty case (who we had also treated and returned to full fitness). George sadly lost his wife a month before finding out their adored cat had been in a road accident, breaking his pelvis and one of his back legs. These were injuries which could be repaired, recovery and progress would have been successful in this case; however, he couldn't afford the surgery and care and the cat wasn't insured. In the end he had to make the heartbreaking decision to let his cat go; seeing a very proud old man sob and look so lonely pulled on every heart string. Although the vet and I managed to hold it together until he left the room, we couldn't stop our tears either. Sometimes (from our point of view) it's only our colleagues who understand how we feel; as clients, rightly so, generally only ever see the professional side.

I thought about George most of the night when I got home, how lonely he must have been feeling and how empty and quiet the house must have seemed. Sadly this is not an isolated case.

Shall I move on? Okay then (but get them insured)!

Grooming

I can hear groans from some people, but animals do need their hair and nails doing too! Roughly every 6–8 weeks depending on the breed (slightly longer for cats), a lot of our clients time it with their own hair appointments. Be thankful you don't have to deal with make-up as well, although I'm sure this will be available somewhere in the world or coming to a store near you soon! As with everything I practise, discuss and teach there is always a point to these things. One may scoff at my terms and care provided, such as facials and pedicures, however teeth <u>need</u> to brushed, ears <u>need</u> to be kept clean and nails (if not worn down naturally), <u>need</u> to be cut. Nails that are not worn down or cut, will eventually curl under and grow into their pads. Imagine trying to walk on that? It must be like walking in stilettos (constantly) that pinch and give you blisters but you won't take them back because they are gorgeous and you feel ace in them.

Many owners are great at looking after their pet's coat and hygiene and realise the necessity of this but I've also lost count of the amount of owners who don't, not on purpose of course but because of a lack of knowledge. Grooming will be discussed in more detail later but to keep your dog or cat's hair looking divine, you need to be aware of how to care for their coat. As I've mentioned, it is breed dependent and also personal choice on how you like them to look. Bear in mind dogs such as Lhasa Apsos, Poodles, Bichon Frises, Shih Tzus and cats such as Persians, Ragdolls, long-haired moggies (basically anything with medium to long hair) have high maintenance requirements. These are all very popular pets but you need to have the time to maintain their coats at home and be aware of the costs involved with professional grooming. If you know you haven't time to sit combing your pet on an evening or don't want to be bothered with having to remember yet another appointment, there are plenty of other suitable pets that are less time consuming e.g. Jack Russell Terriers, Weimaraners, Dalmatians, Mini Dachshunds; and for cats – short-haired moggies, Siamese, Bengals; the list can go on. As with exercise, choose your pet wisely, as to the effort and cost you **can and will** put into them.

Temper Tantrums and Strops!

Many breeds have had bad press for being aggressive – we've all heard the stories. Rather than 'pigeon hole' certain breeds into those that have 'aggressive tendencies', I would advise you to research the breed you are interested in and consult professionals regarding their temperament. Any animal can turn or become aggressive, even the softest of dogs and cats still have their survival instincts and if they feel threatened enough they will use them, this has to be understood by all adults and children.

I've drilled into my children if they pull Michael the Beagle's tail enough times, then he may well turn round and bite them – how else does an animal let you know they are cheesed off! It's the same with cats and they can cause injuries to others very quickly and quite often without any warning. If you are scratched or bitten by a cat it is wise to see your doctor. Cat scratches can cause 'Cat Scratch Flu' producing flu-like symptoms. Cat bites can become infected and form abscesses, this is due to a certain type of bacteria the cat carries in its mouth, mainly on the teeth. When the cat bites, this bacteria penetrates into the skin causing subsequent infection and inflammation. Now you know why cats can end up with abscesses from a cat bite. Often fighting and bites are a result from a disagreement over who's 'turf' they're on!

During one hectic morning of operating and road accidents being admitted, we dealt with many dogs and lots of cats who were all cooperative and behaved well. 'Robert' a police dog, (who is trained to be aggressive and to attack), always required handling in a different way compared to 'normal domestic pets'. For 90% of the time it worked; we managed him without undue stress to him or the staff, the other 10% of the time we wouldn't risk being eaten and would just call his handler in! But even Robert was on top form this particularly morning. Step forward the Chihuahua, this tiny dog put the fear of god into some very experienced staff. Just to get her out of the kennel required me, two grown men and a very large beach towel. At this point we reckoned that Robert was thinking "small man syndrome," I, however was thinking, "Give me Robert any day over this!" Trying to anaesthetise her bordered on ridiculous, but we got there in the end and what a lovely feeling it was when she was asleep!

The point of this story is, my experience (of dealing with hundreds of pets over the years) tells me any pet can be aggressive, dismissive, frightened (this can be shown as aggression also), happy, laid-back or daft and we should never assume or typecast.

The easiest way to try and avoid behavioural issues and temper tantrums is to get the correct training (particularly for dogs) from the earliest age feasible. There are numerous puppy and adult training classes and dog behaviour specialists. As with anything, use common sense, there are a lot of 'wannabes' in this field. It is wise to consult the Association of Pet Dog Trainers or Professional Association of Applied Canine Trainers to source suitably qualified people (see Useful Contacts).

Cats however are more solitary creatures and usually prefer to be on their own, their behaviour and traits are completely different to dogs, with environment and stress factors playing a massive role. Cats (as well as dogs) will also show, dismissive behaviour, aggression, fear, happiness etc. I actually have far more scars on my arms from working with cats than I do from dogs, yet we don't seem to hear about the 'man-eating' fluffy cat half as much as we do about aggressive-type dogs. Be aware, an aggressive cat as a pet is no fun and professional help should be sought as to why it is displaying that type of behaviour.

I do appreciate I am usually seeing these pets outside their normal environments, which from a cat's point of view is mega. But if we have an understanding of our pets' behaviour, how to handle them and train them correctly from a young age (don't forget training the other adults and children in the house too) you are less likely to have problems when they are older – the vets and groomers appreciate it too!

Does Age Matter?

Again your choice should be down to the type of lifestyle you have. Puppies and kittens can be much like babies and incredibly hard work, you thought potty training your two-year-old was hard! Although they are extremely cute and lots of fun, will you think that when your young kitten is hanging off the newly-hung curtains creating clicks galore? Or you are wiping up wee for the tenth time that day (the dog's not the child's!), hopefully the wee is not on your Hungarian goose feather duvet!

A lot of people wouldn't have it any other way. If however you would prefer a pet a little more grown-up, then usually over the age of two years is a good idea or even a senior pet. Technically, senior refers to dogs and cats aged eight years and over, unless it's a large breed dog, then the senior age starts at five years. Just to be clear, a large breed is any dog that, as an adult, will weigh over 25Kg. The rule of thumb here is the smaller the dog the longer they will live. A Yorkshire Terrier can live until they are fifteen for example but a Bull Mastiff or New Foundland will probably only live until about nine years old. There are exceptions of course, my parent's dog JJ, a Giant Schnauzer lived until he was twelve and half (with arthritis and a heart condition). He did amazingly well and this is a great example of owners showing they have a good understanding of their dog, lifestyle, associated illness and what was best for him. Plus he was insured, so any treatment could be carried out without feeling they had to compromise his care because of cost. He is very much missed.

Whether you are new to owning a pet or this is old hat, I never tire of the buzz you feel when you have helped someone and/or their pet. Making a difference is what it is all about and hopefully you have picked up some useful information from this chapter for you to chew over (sorry, I had to use the pun!) even if it's only one point, then that's good enough for me.

Enjoy!

For the main course I would like...

OK, so that's two Mojitos, a Caesar salad with dressing and a bone to finish? Your pooch may lunch with you and friends and be wearing the latest 'must have' but that does not mean they have to eat like you. It is so important to feed the correct diet and the reasons why shall become clearer as you read on.

Before I explain anything else, please remember your pet DOES NOT NEED VARIETY. They do not get bored of their food like we would if we ate the same thing every day – pets don't have that perception of food. No, seriously they don't, they do not give a rats arse whether they are devouring a Panini with Brie and roasted vegetables or Baked Beans on Toast. All they want is their dinner, so they don't feel hungry. Frequently changing their diet and adding extras in can cause tummy problems, skin issues and create 'fussy eaters' not to mention weight disasters. **Start as you mean to go on and stick to it**.

In case you are thinking I am being a wet blanket and a bore, treats can be given but should be used wisely – I will give you some ideas for these but I'm afraid no double-dipped slowly-baked organic cookies for our trendy pets!

The definition of nutrition = A solid or liquid that is capable of nourishing a living being, allowing normal function of cells and promoting life.

The technical bit

Without wishing to remind you of your school years, it is necessary to understand a little about nutrition. This way you can make informed and sensible decisions about what to feed. Believe me, this kind of information is valuable knowledge when you are searching through what is now a huge range of dog and cat diets (the ranges are likely to increase and widen as time goes on) and besides, knowledge is always power!

When I talk about a complete diet I am referring to a diet that contains all the nutrients needed by a particular animal in order to provide nutrition. It is essential the diet you choose does this, as this is the only food they are going to be fed (bar a few treats here and there).

Dogs and cats both require: protein, carbohydrates, fats, vitamins, minerals and water.

The following information is based on adult pets that are healthy, with no illnesses, allergies or intolerances. Apologies if this brings on the Zzzzzzz, but it is worth knowing!

Protein

Protein is needed for tissue growth and repair, great for broken nails! But cartilage, tendons, muscles, skin, hair and antibodies require it too. Protein is one of the most important parts of your pet's food and is made up of chains of amino acids. Pets require proteins from an animal source rather than from plants or cereals.

There are 21 amino acids that are used and they are classed as either essential or non-essential. Each protein has its own combination of essential and non-essential amino acids. The really scrummy part of protein is something called the biological value (BV) which refers to the quality of the protein, determined by the number of essential amino acids the protein contains. A food with a high BV has most or the entire range essential amino acids, a food with low essential amino acids is said to have a low BV.

Foods with a high BV are digested and absorbed by the body far easier, thus less waste has to be carried through the intestines. The good stuff is absorbed into the body, producing better looking hair, muscles and nails, super strong immune systems (spending less time poorly and therefore less time at the vets) and better formed poos (far easier to pick up – bonus!).

The BV also has an impact on how much needs to be fed, low BV protein has to be given in far greater quantities. When choosing your pet food check what is used as the main source of protein. It should be an animal protein with a high BV rather than a vegetable/cereal protein. A food may boast high protein content but quite often the source can be feathers, beaks and other equally not so pleasant bits. This type of protein has a low BV and is not easy for the body to digest and therefore use. As we want our trendy pets to have glowing skin, shiny hair, gorgeous nails, healthy muscles and a superb immune system, we need to remember it is the BV content of protein that is important. The age old rule of quality not quantity applies even to protein!

Foods with a high BV include eggs, chicken, fish (particularly salmon), pork and beef. Check out these labels in Food Image 1 so you know what you are looking for. These are taken from a premium range of food and are the ideal contents and amounts.

Fats – also known as lipids

Fats provide essential energy and also carry the fat soluble vitamins – A, D, E and K. Cats and dogs need at least 1%–2% fat in their diet to be able to absorb these vitamins. As we all know fat makes food taste better (think muesli compared to brioche), which may make for yummy eating but they have to be consumed sensibly to enable them to keep their cool swagger from turning into a walking table.

Fats are made from fatty acids and glycerol and are either saturated or unsaturated (the amount of 'bonds' contained in the fat determines this). Just as there are essential amino acids in protein, there are also essential fatty acids (EFA):

- Linoleic
- Alpha-linolenic
- Arachidonic acid

These are the omega-3 and omega-6 fatty acids that we have heard so much about over recent years regarding our own health. While we might want to take these as supplements, to aid the quest on becoming Britain's brainiest and best behaved, we do not need to supplement our pets as a rule. These EFAs are provided in exactly the right quantities in their 'complete diet'. There may be times however when extra EFAs are needed – they work well for dandruff and dry skin for example. However they need the right versions of the many that are about. Ask your vet or vet nurse about which ones to use – rubbing half a bottle of finest Greek olive oil on their coat just won't cut it I'm afraid!

Carbohydrates

The main source of carbohydrates is plants and can be divided into four groups but basically these sugars (e.g. fruit) and starch (e.g. rice) are used as a glucose source, to provide energy, heat and storage of energy as glycogen and fat. Carbohydrates provide 40%–50% of energy in dogs and 30% of energy in cats. Cats require lower levels of carbohydrates as they are unable to metabolise large amounts and derive most of their energy from proteins and fat. Carb-free diets may be fantastic and work well for people (although personally I love my bread far too much to be a carb-free kinda girl!) but not for dogs and cats.

Vitamins

Another element of the diet that needs careful consideration is vitamins. Excess and deficiencies can cause more problems than you think – see Table F1.

Vitamins A, D, E and K are fat-soluble and need fat to be carried and absorbed; excess of these vitamins is stored in the body.

Vitamins B and C are water soluble. Excess of these two are excreted in the urine. As the body cannot store these vitamins (unlike the fat-soluble ones) Vitamin B and C have to be provided within their daily diet. These will already be in their complete diet, so do not need supplementing.

Micro-minerals (trace elements)

This is another part of the diet which can often be overlooked but just as important, as they aid maintenance of the metabolic process. Again, excesses and deficiencies can cause problems – see Table F1.

Micro-minerals include, selenium, iron, zinc, manganese.

TABLE F1

Nutritional excess and deficiencies in dogs and cats.

These are some of the common nutrient imbalances
and is by no means exhaustive!

Nutrient	A deficiency can cause:	An excess can cause:
Protein	Skin sores, dull dry coat, brittle nails, loss of muscle definition. In puppies and kittens can lead to poor growth and joint/bone issues.	None reported
Fat	Weight losses as energy levels are not met. A lack of the EFAs can result in anaemia, hair loss and liver issues.	Obesity and therefore the problems associated with obesity.
Carbohydrates	None reported unless they are not receiving their energy from protein and fat.	Digestive disorders
Vitamin A	This can occur in cats fed a vegetarian diet or dogs fed offal diets. Decreased immune response, sore, dry, itchy skin. 'Night blindness, crusty sores around the nostrils and problems with bone development.	This can occur in cats fed a liver diet, and in dogs and cats that are given too much cod liver oil. Results seen can be pain, lameness and bone/joint stiffness (especially in the cat's neck), liver damage, weakness and anorexia i.e. your pet won't eat.
Calcium and phosphorus	These two are very important and work together as a ratio. Too low results in bone being reabsorbed by the body causing walking or standing problems, pain, weak bones and fractures. Problems with the parathyroid glands.	In puppies, especially the large breeds, too much calcium results in bone and joint abnormalities e.g. hip dysplasia. Crystals or stones may appear in urine (cats).
Taurine	Blindness (central retinal degeneration), heart disease – dilated cardiomyopathy. Reduced growth rate. Reproduction issues.	None reported
Arachidonic acid	Poor, dry skin and hair. Problems with the reproductions systems (male and female). Problems with the immune system.	None reported

Water

Your pet's body loses water every day from urine, faeces, breathing, and sweating. Sweating though is not really an issue for pets, they only sweat from their pads and noses and even then it is not that much. How lucky are they?! However water HAS to be taken in every day to replace these losses and to keep the body hydrated, this is done in two ways:

1. Via drinking water – tap water is fine, save the bottled, filtered, collected from organic rocks type of water, for you!

2. Via food – wet food (tinned/pouches/trays) have approximately 70% moisture content, dry food has approximately 10% moisture content. A pet on dried food will always drink far more water than a pet on wet food and should be allowed to do so.

See below for examples of food labels showing the ideal content of dog and cat food.

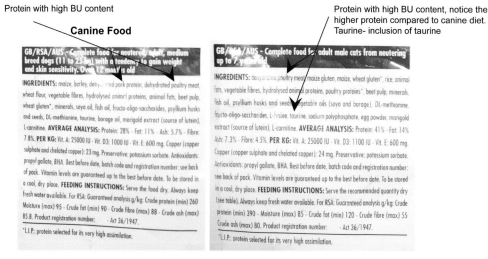

With Kind permission from Royal Canin

Vegetarian diets

As you have being paying attention! You will know the protein source for pets is of animal origin. Cats derive most of their energy from protein and require 2–3 times more as an adult, this is why a vegetarian diet for cats in particular, is really not a good idea. See the very important information paragraph for more on this. It is possible to feed your pet a vegetarian diet (there are certainly some available), as long as all the nutrients required from meat have being added in. Discuss this with your vet or vet nurse first before swapping them onto these diets. Please take a moment to think whether this is your personal choice and view or your pet's.

Milk

Cow's milk can cause upset tummies – anything from loose poo to diarrhoea galore. Once puppies and kittens are weaned, their bodies don't have the ability to digest milk; lactose (a milk sugar) is one of the main culprits. They may well love the white stuff but their bodies don't, as it is just too difficult to digest and causes havoc with tummies and intestines.

They don't need milk and ideally both dogs and cats should not be given this. Cat milk is available, which is lactose free. The trendiest and safest option is not to give milk, of any kind, in the first place. (I can feel half the cat population giving me the evil eye now!)

Very important information

Cats are obligate carnivores, meaning – they have to eat meat. Two extra requirements are added into feline diets:

1. Taurine – an essential amino acid (protein group). Needed for normal vision, cardiac function, proper function of the immune and nervous systems

2. Arachidonic acid – an essential fatty acid (fat group). Needed to maintain the skin, hair and proper function of the reproductive and immune systems.

These are derived from animal meat but are lost during processing the food and the body cannot make them, hence why they have to be added in. This is why feeding a cat a vegetarian diet is a no no (technically I suppose, these could be produced and added in).

Although an excess of taurine is non-toxic, a deficiency causes big problems – see Food Table 1.

A deficiency of arachidonic acid also has its effects but these can take some months to be seen – see Food Table 1.

The needs for these two nutrients are the reason it is essential a cat is fed 'cat food'.

Obvious, you may well be thinking, but unfortunately I have seen cases over the years where owners, for example, have fed only tuna or only dog food to their cat. Commonly justified by 'it's the only thing they will eat' (taurine and arachidonic acid are only added into cat diets).

I remember one cat in particular who, by the time the owner brought him to us, could barely see and unfortunately had raging heart disease. The heart disease (caused by a lack of taurine) is what we call a dilated cardiomyopathy, basically the wall of the heart (the muscle) becomes thinner and thinner and the chambers inside become bigger and bigger. As the heart muscle is too thin, it struggles to pump the blood through the chambers of the heart and out towards the rest of the body, made twice as hard as the chambers are also too big. The result? Heart disease and failure begins. In the above case the cat had to be put to sleep, all because he was fed dog food.

OK that's the first class of the day over with! Go grab a latte and Danish and settle down for the next one, we'll allow this treat – we need carbs and fat for energy remember and concentrating requires energy!

Life stage and breed diets

The lovely pet food companies are now widening our choices but trying to personalise it at the same time. Age, breed, neutering, illness, weight, pregnancy and activity all influence our pets' nutritional requirements. Having a diet all made up for you, specifically for your pet's needs, fits into our fast-moving lifestyles perfectly. It's one less thing to think about, whilst knowing you are providing the best type of nutrition for them. This is undeniably reflected in their appearance, their toilet habits and general health.

1. *Life stage diets*

The diets briefly mentioned below contain all the components noted earlier, with appropriate variations.

Puppy and kitten – These are energy dense, increased in protein and minerals. For large breed puppies, energy is lower to prevent excessive weight gain, plus calcium and phosphorous are controlled to aid bone formation and joints. If your puppy will weigh over 25Kg as an adult, they need to be fed a large breed puppy diet. Large breeds are prone to bone and joint problems, therefore they need different levels of nutrients like calcium and must not gain weight too quickly whilst growing.

Adults – These contain all the standard amounts for maintenance. Again if your dog weighs over 25Kg they need to be fed a large breed diet.

Neutered pets – After neutering, your pet is at a higher risk of putting weight on. Basically their calorie requirements are lower and metabolism is slower. If they eat the same amount as they did prior to neutering, they will gain weight. 'Neutered diets' control the amount of energy and allow for the metabolic changes of the body following neutering, therefore helping to maintain an ideal weight. Alternatively a 'light' version of the diet may be fed.

Pregnancy – Pregnant bitches and queens should be fed puppy or kitten diets, they should remain on this during pregnancy and whilst they are feeding their young.

Working – e.g. racing Greyhounds, require higher energy and digestibility from their food.

Senior – These are reduced in energy and protein but vitamins are increased. Organs start to slow down as they get older and their function can start to deteriorate. Senior diets allow for this, making it as easy as possible for the body to digest and use the nutrients.

2. *Breed Specific diets*

There are now a number of diets for various breeds of dogs and cats e.g. Shih Tzu, Poodle, Chihuahua, Labrador, German shepherd, Persian, British Short Hair, Siamese and many more.

I personally love these, very 21st century! Most breeds tend to have a disposition of some kind, i.e. prone to certain problems or disease. The breed specific diets target these and aid prevention of them occurring in the first place. Usually each breed specific diet targets three or more issues.

Attention to the shape of the biscuit has not being overlooked either and is different for each breed e.g. almond shapes, squares, round with a hole in the middle, no heart-shaped ones yet though! This is to aid them actually picking the food up and chewing it properly, a problem faced by many 'flat faced' breeds. They are a complete diet as well – double bonus!

Examples of some predispositions and breeds:

Weight gain – Labradors, Cocker Spaniels, Pugs. These diets are formulated to try and maintain an ideal weight.

Skin problems – West Highland White Terrier, Bulldogs, German Shepherds. These diets are formulated to support the skin barrier and promote and maintain healthy skins and coats.

Heart function – Cavalier King Charles, Boxers, Persians. These diets are formulated to support and maintain heart function.

Dental disease – British Short Hair cats, Shih Tzus, Yorkshire terriers. These diets are formulated to help maintain dental care and reduce the build-up of tartar.

Joint problems – German Shepherds, Great Danes, Maine Coon. These diets are formulated to aid and support joints and mobility.

Digestive problems – German Shepherds, Siamese, Great Dane. These diets are formulated to maintain often very sensitive digestive systems.

All the breeds mentioned (and more that I haven't) have a specific diet available for them by Royal Canin and are well worth considering feeding to your adult dog or cat. Some puppy and kitten breed diets have being added to the range too.

Currently Royal Canin and Eukanuba produce these, with Royal Canin being the originators and certainly providing the larger range. Superb information is available on their websites or speak to them (see Useful Contacts) regarding further information. These people lurve their nutrition!

Dry versus wet food

The most important thing here is, yes you guessed it – they must be a complete diet! To be fair, most are, but mixers (the food type not the tonic for your gin!) are still available, as are lots and lots of complementary foods.

Mixers are dry biscuits which need to be 'mixed' with the wet food of the same brand. The problem here is you need to ensure you get the ratios right to provide all the correct levels of nutrients. Not only do you have to purchase two types of food, albeit they can be cheaper, you need to be able to store them, and as well as this some pets do not find them palatable (despite their cheaper cost if they don't eat them, it's a waste of money).

Complementary foods are just that, and must not be used or thought of as a complete diet. They are often used as a way of giving your pet a treat. Some are in a typical treat form, rawhide chews for example; others are sold in small tins, trays or pouches. There are some fairly swanky sounding ones too, using foods such as Alaskan salmon and Tiger prawns but be warned, they tend to have a high fat and salt content. Complete wet food diets are sold in tins, pouches and trays, these are fairly easy to store and most dogs and cats find them very palatable. They can work out expensive and not as convenient as dried food. They generally make dental disease worse and certainly don't aid preventative dental care – See chapter, 'Are Those your Own?' for more on this.

Complete dried foods are available for both dogs and cats and are far more convenient and better for their teeth than wet foods. Some may not find these as palatable but try and persevere if this is the type of food you would like them to eat.

See Appendix 2 for 'How to change your pet's diet'.

Presentation!

Presentation of your pet's food is actually pretty important, particularly where cats are concerned. Here are ten pointers about serving your pet's main course (whether these are to the standards of 'The Ivy' is a different matter!). I'm not talking about a dinner plate the size of a half a table, that's white with a tiny amount of food in the middle!

1. Feed puppies and kittens from shallow, wide bowls or saucers.

2. Cats prefer to eat from wide shallow bowls as these don't squash their whiskers while eating. Cats use their whiskers to judge 'widths' of spaces e.g. can they sneak through that narrow gap to get away from the street bully! They do not like having their whiskers interfered with.

3. Some cats prefer metal or ceramic bowls over plastic ones, the plastics can give off a certain smell that they do not like. Saying that, some cats and dogs don't like the clinking noise that stainless steel bowls can make, their collar tags hitting the bowl while they're eating can create this noise too. Adjust the bowl accordingly.

4. For elderly or poor-sighted pets, use shallow wide bowls that are non-slip and keep them in the same place so they know where to find their food and water.

5. Fresh water should be available at all times – no ice!

6. Clean food bowls daily, hard crusted food not only encourages bacterial growth but will put some pets off eating. Most metal and some of the ceramic ones can go in the dishwasher – Yey!

7. Feeding and drinking bowls should not be placed near a cat's litter tray or toileting area. They really do not like this and quite often will not eat – well would you?

8. Most dogs and cats do not like food that is cold. If you keep opened food in the fridge remove it and warm to room temperature first.

9. In warm weather remove uneaten food. I had an incident this summer where I had left the remainder of my own cat's food out, for about 30 minutes. To my horror a fly had already laid its eggs in there, so that meant little tiny baby maggots all over it – it was just foul and sooo not chic!

10. Use the feeding guides provided on your chosen food, regarding how much to feed. Always measure it out (do not guess). If they are over or under weight, feed the amount for what they should weigh, not what they actually do.

As a quick summary, my four rules of thumb are:

1.   Feed species specific e.g. don't feed a cat on dog food, purely tuna or similar.

2.   Feed a complete diet, make sure the diet you choose is a 'complete diet' and not a treat or mixer. Leftovers from our meals or meat from the butcher do not constitute a complete diet either.

3.   Feed for age and/or lifestyle or breed, if appropriate; and feed the amount for the weight they should be, not what they actually weigh.

4.   You get what you pay for (but you don't need me to remind of you of this rule!). The very cheap brands of food use cheap low grade ingredients that frequently change, remember the feathers and beaks? These brands will use the cheapest ingredients available at the time of making that particular batch. When they come to make the next batch, often the 'cheap' ingredients have changed e.g. pork might be cheaper initially but beef is cheaper next time and so on. This can explain some irritated tummies and why your pet, all of sudden, won't eat a food they have being happily troughing away at. The more expensive/premium brands have a 'fixed formula' and adhere to at every batch made, i.e. their ingredients and quality do not change. Always feed the best diet you can afford, we apply this rule to clothes, shoes and make up, food should be no different.

The dangers of being overweight

Some factors for example, neutering, breed type, age (risk increases with age), sex type – females are more likely to gain than males (typical!) un- accounted for treats or feeding them ad libitum all make weight gain more of a problem.

A pet is classed as obese if they are 15% over their ideal body weight, this happens because the calorie intake exceeds their expenditure for a period of time. If your pet is overweight, you need to sort this out for them, it isn't funny or cute, it's serious, just as it is with humans.

Before embarking on any sort of weight loss programme, your vet must examine your pet first to ensure they are well. Certain illnesses – Diabetes mellitus, hypothyroidism (underactive thyroid), steroid therapies and some anti-epileptic drugs can all increase weight. These diseases need to be ruled out first or, addressed if they are discovered.

There is no doubt excess weight shortens their life by causing problems and illness such as:

•   Heart disease and failure.

•   Increased cancer risk.

- Kidney related disease.

- High blood pressure.

- Stress on the joints is increased, making conditions like arthritis much worse.

- Changes in metabolism effecting glucose and insulin secretion.

- Increased risk of complications if a general anaesthetic is needed.

- Certain breeds are more likely to develop urinary crystals.

Keep them fit and healthy by feeding the correct diet and amount. Keep treats to a minimum and use exercise and games to burn the calories off.

Weight programmes can be initiated by your or vet nurse once their health has being given the all clear.

Trick or healthy treat

Through experience and research, the experts tell us that feeding treats to our pets is more about how it makes you feel as owner (giving your pet something it enjoys), rather than the pet actually wanting or needing it.

Use these appropriately, not because they look cute, deserve one or because you are having one! You might like to have a mini muffin while 'Corrie' is on but they don't need one too!

They can be useful as rewards and aids to training but use ones from the ideas below, not big chunks of cheese or a selection of continental cold meats!

Healthy treats and game ideas

A portion taken from their daily diet allowance – this is the best idea.

Ice cubes – These are fantastic, they contain zero calories and most dogs seem to love the ice and play with them too, keeping them occupied at the same time. Make from good old plain water and don't put any of the cute accessories in that will freeze in the middle, like pink hearts or little plastic spiders in the case of my son. Needless to say my well-deserved drink that day was ruined! I now cheat and buy bags of ice cubes for me and Michael the Beagle from the supermarket – nice one!

James Wellbeloved treats – Pure indulgence for cats or Pure incentives for dogs. These tubs of 25g treats contain approximately 100 Kcal, the source of protein used in these is also fab.

Here are the calorie requirements of an average dog and cat along with the calorie contents of some common treats, as kindly supplied by Royal Canin:

A 15Kg dog should consume approximately 1,040 Kcal per day
A 5Kg cat should consume approximately 250 Kcal per day

1 slice of bread with margarine and cheese 180 Kcal
1 slice of cake 140 Kcal
1 slice of bread with paté 130 Kcal
1 cooked potato 80 Kcal
1 piece of cheese (20g) 75 Kcal
1 slice sausage/salami (25g) 75 Kcal
1 glass semi-skimmed milk (150ml) 70 Kcal
1 biscuit (on average) 55 Kcal
1 rice cake 35 Kcal
¼ apple 15 Kcal
1 piece of carrot < 5 Kcal
1 slice of cucumber < 5 Kcal

There are lots of treats to buy which no doubt they will love but if you are not sure of the calorie content is best not to give them. Treats and chews such as pigs' ears are well documented to be a source of Salmonella (Finley et al 2008). Trust me, you don't need a dose of salmonella doing the rounds!

Healthy treats or a portion of their daily diet can be used in treat balls or puzzle-type treat games to help relieve boredom, as they have to figure out how to get the treats out – do you think we could use these for children or is that a cruel idea?!

Treat balls can also be used to feed the meals from – brilliant! This keeps them occupied and takes them longer to eat the meal, which is far better than wolfing it down in 30 seconds. Great for cats but they like to be able to see their food, so you use a clear or 'see through' treat ball or adapt an empty drinks bottle.

Cats love to hunt, hide some of the healthy treats or diet around the house for them to find.

A portion of the diet or the healthy treats can be thrown about in the garden, cats and dogs can then go off 'hunting' to find them all.

Use a torch or laser pen to play catch the light – popular with cats and young children too!

Throw balls or their favourite toy for them to chase up and down the stairs.

Bone appetite!

When to see the vet

- Not eating at all.

- Eating more or less than normal.

- Not drinking at all.

- Drinking more or less than normal.

- Persistent diarrhoea or vomiting.

- Regurgitation of food – this is different to vomiting. Vomiting is a forced action with retching. Regurgitation doesn't present with retching or heaving, often looks like a sausage containing undigested food.

- Itchy skin.

- Underweight.

- Overweight.

- Bloating of the stomach after eating/ exercise, especially with unproductive retching, discomfort and breathing problems – this is an emergency.

Ears what it's about

We all remember those awful earache moments from childhood, I certainly remember scarves being wrapped around my head, the pink medicine and hot water bottles.

Our dogs and cats are unfortunately no different, except scarves, pink medicine and mummy cuddles don't really work on them.

As with anything, we need to understand the normal before we know what it is that's abnormal.

The normal ear

A normal healthy ear (see Murphy's ear below) should be a nice pink colour with no obnoxious smells, discharges or bleeding. The ear canal should be free from hair and wax and the ear pinna (ear flap) should not have a 'ripple effect' that feels hard nor should it feel 'squashy'. Your pet should not show signs of itchy ears or head tilts. If your pet demonstrates these healthy characteristics, excellent, they have a nice pair of ears! Their ears should therefore be able to perform the two functions they are meant to do, that is, hearing and balance.

To be technical there are three sections to the ear (just like ours); the external ear, the middle ear and the inner ear, (see anatomical image opposite).The external ear consists of the pinna, the ear canals and the ear drum (a very thin membrane not the steel or beating kind!). The ear drum separates the external ear and middle ear.

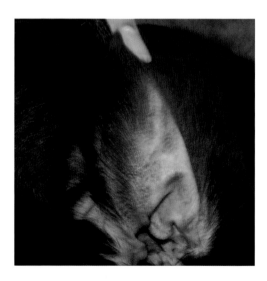

The middle ear is an air-filled cavity containing three tiny bones and a tube that connects the nose and throat with the ear. This air-filled cavity ensures the pressure in the ear stays the same as outside air pressure. You are correct in thinking that this is the reason our ears 'pop', do funny things and cause lots of children to scream on aeroplanes, as the pressure inside the aircraft is different. The function of the middle ear is to amplify sounds. The inner ear is right at the end within the skull. This contains lots of bony bits, tubes and fluid which together detect different sound frequencies and are also responsible for balance.

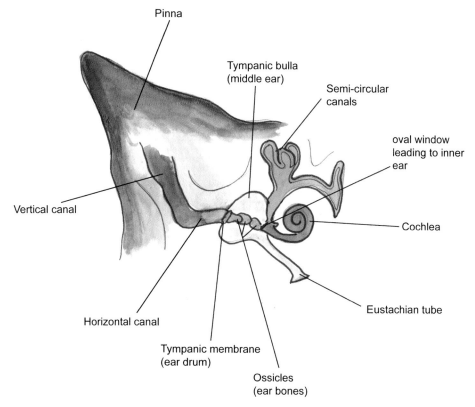

Ear disease can occur in any of the three sections, although inflammation of the external ear (Otitis Externa) is the most common, this is what we think of as an 'ear infection and inflammation'. Otitis Media (inflammation of the middle ear) and Otitis Interna (inflammation of the inner ear) are usually caused by an extension of Otitis Externa.

I have being unfortunate enough to personally experience middle ear disease and I would have quite happily ripped my own head off, it hurt that much and made me feel incredibly ill. The advantage of being a human though is that I can use my best poorly voice (including tears) to blag the earliest appointment possible with a doctor. For our pets however, we need to be their eyes and ears so we know when something is wrong and can start them back on the road to health again. The thought of a pet having to endure what I did, unnoticed, upsets me.

I appreciate disease and illnesses are often out of our hands but the more we keep the ears healthy the less likely they are to get ear disease, which is great for your pet and your pennies.

What makes pets more prone to ear disease?

Many pets tend to have a hard time with their ears (it seems this rate is higher in dogs than in cats). There are a few different factors which instigate ear disease, the treatment will therefore be dependent on the cause. Please remember if only the symptoms are treated and the original cause of the ear disease is not, then the disease and its symptoms will either continue or produce repeated episodes.

All of the following have the potential to cause Otitis Externa. 'Ears' what our pets are up against!

- The <u>anatomy</u> of the cat and dog ear is different to ours. They have much longer vertical and horizontal car canals that join (nearly) at a right angle halfway down – see diagram Ear 2.

- <u>Breed</u>: Certain breeds e.g. Poodles, have hairy ears, hair builds up in the vertical canal until it is removed by plucking. If this is not removed, ear discomfort and infection is more likely. I have dealt with dogs that have never had their ears plucked and the amount of hair within the canal can be quite unbelievable. Ever accused your dog of temporary hearing? Check their ears first!

  Men with hairy ears, be thankful of that nose and ear trimmer at least you don't have to pluck yours!

- <u>Shape of the ears</u>: The ear cartilage that supports the pinna determines its shape; some are 'floppy' like in Cocker Spaniels and some are 'upright' (to collect sounds) like in German Shepherds. 'Floppy ears' have decreased airflow within the ear canals, this can increase the chances of ear discomfort and disease. The ear canals tend to be warmer and have increased moisture which is perfect for yeasts and bacteria to grow and cause infection. 'Upright ears' have better air flow and therefore less heat and moisture in the ear canals, so tend to have fewer problems.

- <u>Activities</u> they undertake such as swimming can lead to bacteria within the ear canals causing ear disease and infection. Foraging in undergrowth can lead to small foreign bodies becoming lodged and stuck in the canals. Grass seeds very commonly do this and cause inflammation and subsequent infection, not to mention irritation to your pet.

- <u>Parasites</u> – in particular Otodectes Cynotis (the Ear Mite). Ear mites are very contagious and can pass between mother and offspring, between the same species and between dog, cat and ferret – fortunately though, our ears are safe! These tiny non-burrowing mites (i.e. they live on top of the skin rather than in it) are itchy itchy itchy and must drive pets insane.

These are only just visible to the naked eye, if you remove a piece of wax/dirt from their ear and look at it carefully, you can see little white dots moving about (just!).

- Bacterial infection – often these infecting bugs are secondary to another condition. This is why it is important to treat the cause and not just the symptoms.

- Fungal infections – the most commonly found fungi in the ear, although certainly not fun to have, is called Malassezia. Again this is often secondary to another condition and the original cause needs to be treated as well.

- Allergic skin disease – allergies seem to be everywhere causing all sorts of problems – ears are no different I'm afraid.

Just for interest:

Hereditary and congenital defects – OK, what's the difference between hereditary and congenital? Give up? Alright I'll tell! A hereditary condition is passed on through genes. Congenital defects are conditions or defects present at birth, such as an umbilical hernia, cleft palate. More often than not congenital defects are also hereditary. Some interesting examples of hereditary ear conditions include:

The Scottish Fold cat – This breed of cat has folded ear tips.

Deafness either in one or both ears – Common in Dalmatians, White Boxers, White English Bull Terriers, and white cats. Breeders are trying to ensure that these 'deafness' genes are not passed on to the next generation – I say modern medicine should look into this for certain human types!

Sometimes the signs of ear problems are slight and can be missed, until that is, the ear disease is in full roaring infection mode or the ear mites have taken over residence with no signs of moving out.

Signs of ear disease

- Redness.
- Heat.
- Inflammation and or ulceration on the inside of the ear.
- Discharges from the ear, including pus and blood. A small amount of dark brown wax is normal, thick black wax or a build-up of wax however is not.
- Obnoxious smells.
- Irritation, this may be demonstrated in a few ways – scratching, using their paws to rub their ears, scratching or rubbing other parts of the

head (just like when we can't find the itch!), rubbing their ears on floors or furniture, shaking their heads.

- Other pets may lick the infected ear of the dog or cat.
- Pain – again this will manifest itself differently depending on your pet. Signs of pain include becoming submissive or aggressive, 'pawing at the ear', not eating, generally uninterested, lethargy.
- An ear pinna that feels 'squashy' likes it's filled with water.
- Flickering eyes (pupils moving side to side) – seen mainly in Otitis Interna.
- The head tilting to one side – seen mainly in Otitis Interna.
- Third eyelid protrusion and a constricted pupil on the affected side – seen mainly in Otitis Interna.

So how do we get it to go away?

Once you have seen the vet and they have made a diagnosis and identified the cause, you will more than likely be sent home with medication. Now, depending on the cause and severity this can take various forms. This following list is certainly not exhaustive but covers the basic and common ear treatments:

- Topical ear antibiotics – these are drops placed directly in the ear canal and can be used to treat infection, inflammation and mites.
- Systemic antibiotics – these antibiotics are usually tablets taken orally or given by injection and can be used to treat any infection and inflammation (external, middle and inner).
- Flea spot on treatments – some of the prescription flea spot on treatments can be used to treat and prevent ear mites.
- Anti inflammatory drugs – these are sometimes given either as tablets, liquid or as an injection, these drugs provide pain relief and help reduce the inflammation.
- Shampoo – you may be given special shampoo to use if the ear infection is secondary to another condition, which can often be related to the skin on their bodies.
- Removal of foreign bodies. This has to be performed under general anaesthetic and your pet is likely to have medication to use at home as well.
- Flushing their ears – this is performed under general anaesthetic, fluid such as sterile saline is often used and this removes all sorts of wax, debris and blockages. Antibiotics may also be applied after flushing them and you may have medication to use at home as well.

- For chronic ear conditions there are various types of surgery they can have, which your vet would discuss with you.

Ears something interesting!

Aural haematomas (a collection of blood under the skin in the ear pinna). I've mentioned 'squashy' ear pinnas a couple of times, these occur when blood leaks out of the blood vessels into the ear pinna. These are commonly seen in ear disease as constant shaking of the head causes trauma to the blood vessels, allowing blood to leak out and pool in the ear pinna. Aural haematomas may be treated non surgically by draining and administering medications or, they can be surgically repaired. The hard, ripple effect ear pinna I mentioned, occurs following aural haematomas that have not being treated.

I need to mention ear drums, if the ear drum is ruptured i.e. has a hole in it, then most ear cleaners and some topical ear antibiotics cannot be used as it will make the condition worse. If the ear is showing signs of any infection, **stop** any ear cleaning you are doing at home until you have seen your vet. Most of the time the ear drum can be visualised by looking down the ear with an auroscope; severe ear disease or infection however, may obscure the view or prevent it from being seen at all.

We hear it all the time 'do not use cotton buds to clean ears'; this is as true for pets as it is for us but why when it is so much easier? Apart from running the danger of pushing wax or debris further down the canal, causing increased irritation and compromising their hearing, you can cause significant damage to the ear drum and the inner ear.

Piercing the ear drum (and not with a pretty diamond stud!) is really easy to do with a cotton bud. Although it does repair itself, there is discomfort and hearing problems until it does so. Horner's Syndrome is a condition of the inner ear which can occur following overzealous ear cleaning, usually with those good old cotton buds.

Basically the sympathetic nerve supply to the head passes close to the middle ear; if this is damaged during the ear-cleaning process it can cause this condition which presents with the following symptoms on the affected side (possibly how one may look after a few too many on a Saturday night as well!):

- Head tilt.
- The pupil becomes constricted (smaller) while the pupil in the other eye remains normal size.
- The third eyelid (a membrane in the corner of the eye, usually not visible) protrudes.

With time and treatment they will recover from this but best not to cause it in the first place – so, 'Step away from the cotton buds'!

How do we prevent ear disease?

To keep their ears squeaky clean, follow the following tips:

1. Check the ears weekly, it's good to know what is 'normal' for your pet, this will allow any infections to be picked up as early as possible.

2. Clean the ears weekly – See Appendix 6.

3. If they are a water-loving dog, clean their ears after each swimming episode. If infection is present they will have to stay away from the water until the all-clear is given by your vet.

4. If you have a dog that requires hair removal from the canal (many do) ensure this is done every 6–8 weeks. This is usually incorporated within their 6–8 weekly haircuts or grooming. Any good groomer will do this as routine – but check they have been done.

5. Use treatments regularly that prevent and treat ear mites – your vet or veterinary nurse will be able to discuss these with you.

6. If they have long hair on their ears, keep them knot-free and free from food and other debris. Things like these can hurt and irritate them and force them to start itching at the ear and shaking their heads.

7. Prevent self-interference. If they have a sore ear, preventing them from trying to itch or rub it is key. This also includes preventing other pets from licking their ears. This information is actually key to any wound or sore they might have and is not just limited to the ears. I must hear the next comment at least once a day, "he's licking it better". **No he isn't**. He is licking or rubbing because it is sore, irritating or painful. By letting them, or others, lick the ears or any sore area they are making it worse. As you will now know from the information earlier (nod your head please!), moist warm skin and sores are perfect for bacteria and/or fungi to grow, therefore they are encouraging this growth.

    If the skin is red, grazed or open then it will take much longer to heal as the licking or rubbing action is causing constant trauma to the skin. Thus making it more painful, they lick more, bacteria sets it, they lick more, becomes more painful – you get the picture. See Appendix 3 on ways to prevent self-interference.

Sorry what was that? I didn't quite hear you!

Things to see the vet about

We now know what the ear should look like so if you spot some or all of the following signs, it's off to the vets you go (I ho, I ho!):

- Redness of the ear.

- Heat in and around the ear.

- Inflammation and or ulceration on the inside of the ear.

- Discharges from the ear, including pus and blood. A small amount of dark brown wax is normal, thick black wax or a build-up of wax however is not.

- Obnoxious smells coming from the ear.

- Irritation, this may be demonstrated in a few ways, scratching, using their paws to rub their ears, scratching or rubbing other parts of the head (just like when we can't find the itch!) rubbing their ears on floors or furniture, shaking their heads.

- Pain – again this will manifest itself differently depending on your pet. Signs of pain include becoming submissive or aggressive, 'pawing at the ear', not eating, generally uninterested, lethargy.

- An ear pinna that feels 'squashy' likes it's filled with water.

- Flickering eyes (nystagmus).

- The head tilting to one side, third eyelid protrusion, and a constricted pupil on the affected.

Are those your own?

So their breath stinks, they don't floss and their teeth are certainly not pearly white. Essentially, care of our pets' teeth is the same as for us humans. If we didn't brush our teeth and take preventative action, then ours would end up looking the same. Unfortunately, this is the case for 80% of dogs and 70% of cats over the age of 3 years and no, we can't whiten them or replace them with veneers!

Dental disease is perhaps one of the most common preventable problems seen in our pets today, which can lead to smelly breath, bleeding gums, difficulty in eating, mouth abscesses, illness and pain, not to mention the expense when treatment is required.

In the wild, the animal's natural diet of meat, bones and other tissues (from their captured prey) act as a very good oral care regime. As our pets are now domesticated and not out hunting all day, oral care and hygiene is down to the owner. Prevention is the absolute key to keeping dental disease under control.

So what goes on in their mouths to cause dental disease, and what are the signs?

Bacteria is present in its thousands in the mouth which increases all the time, for example after eating. If the bacteria is not removed in some way, (ideally by brushing) then bacteria continues to multiply and problems begin. Bacteria causes a sequence of events within the mouth, usually in the following pattern:

1. Bacteria collects just under the gum line (the area where the gum meets the tooth). Once there are sufficient numbers of bacteria, the gum will start to develop a red line called gingivitis (inflammation of the gum) this will in turn become more severe causing increased redness of the gums, increased inflammation, bleeding and pain.

2. The normally white-coloured enamel becomes covered in plaque and will start to stain a yellow/brown colour.

3. Bacteria then mixes with substances within the saliva such as calcium, causing the plaque to turn into thick hard tartar. These three stages continually repeat, increasing the amounts of tartar and gingivitis. Disease of the ligaments and bone, which hold the teeth in place, shortly follows. This can lead to: loose teeth, tooth loss, pain, abscesses, gum recession and exposure of the tooth's roots.

Bad breath (halitosis) by the way, is all the bacteria within the mouth and more importantly, under the gum line. It is also worth mentioning here that bad breath can also be a sign of other illnesses. Different illnesses create different smells and don't smell the same as halitosis. It is always advisable to have this checked out with your vet to ensure you are taking the right course of action. Bad breath maybe one of the first signs you notice – your pet might be blissfully unaware that they have the worst breath in the world, but we definitely aren't!

Staining and tartar can only be removed by using an ultrasonic scale (the same way in which ours are cleaned at the dentist). As dogs and cats will not sit still with their mouth open, general anaesthesia invariably has to be used. Giving your pet a general anaesthetic is not without risks, particularly if they are elderly or poorly. Your vet may even decide that your pet should not have the dental work performed if the risk to your pet is considered too high, leaving them with sore and smelly mouths. The expense for dental work can run into hundreds of pounds, depending on how long it takes and the type of work that needs to be done. Although it may only take 15 minutes to scale and polish our teeth, this is not the case for pets! Can you image a cat with a painful mouth sitting there for up to an hour while we X-ray the mouth, remove teeth, scale and polish, all under a local anaesthetic? No I can't either – I'd rather take my defiant toddler to the dentist than suffer that!

If your pet has had a scale and polish and possibly teeth removed, then some sort of oral care is essential, otherwise, those lovely white teeth will go back to how they looked within 12 months and the procedure may have to be repeated. With all that in mind, surely it's far better to introduce some sort of dental care regime at home to prevent each stage reaching the next and therefore breaking the cycle.

What can we do?

Brushing:

The gold standard in dental care is to brush your pet's teeth daily with an animal toothpaste. Human toothpaste is not meant for swallowing, the high fluoride content can cause an upset stomach in your pet, plus the flavour of human toothpaste is not always well received by your pet, they tend to prefer the very yummy flavours like poultry and fish (come on, it's better than that bad breath surely?).

Always try and choose toothpaste with an enzyme system within it to help break down the bacteria. Various toothbrushes are available from finger ones to dual-ended ones (see image on p37); the choice will be yours and your pet's preference. Personally, I use the dual-ended one in almost every case (apart from on my own cat who bit me when I brushed his – I now use the dental gel described later!).

See Appendix 1 for 'how to brush your pet's teeth'.

Most of us are already meeting ourselves coming backwards whilst hitting our heads on all those balls we juggle, how an earth do you fit daily brushing in for the dog as well? Don't worry, I said I was going to be realistic, there are many alternatives to try. It is far better to do something rather than nothing – don't give up!

Chewing

Chewing is the next best thing to brushing; there are many dental chews available but take care, some are really high in calories. Like the toothpaste options, choose ones that have an enzyme system within it to help break down the bacteria. There are also many dental toys available, some have grooves in them and it is a good idea to fill these grooves with either a toothpaste or dental gel.

Oral gels

Special gels (not the super strength 'I will never move again' hair-type gel!) are available that you can brush or rub onto the gums (some pets may tolerate this better than a brush) and cats can lick the gel from their nose or paw. These work very well as the enzymes within the gel help to break down the bacteria and some owners find them more user-friendly.

Mouthwash

Mouthwashes – see image on p38 – may be squirted directly into the mouth and are not of fire-breathing dragon strength! These are really easy to squirt in and can be used as often as you like. A relatively new product can be added into their drinking water, such as Vet Aquadent (Virbac Animal Health) both of these coat the enamel and help prevent plaque sticking to the surface, which helps the fight against bacteria and freshen breath. For pets that will not tolerate any sort of dental care or who will not chew, use the option of the drinking water additive as it is a very 'hands off' method and easily fits into our schedules (no excuses!).

Diet

Your pet's diet also plays a role. Wet food (tinned meat/pouches) tends to stick to the teeth making the problem worse. If no oral care is available, the remnants of the food fester away on and in between the teeth, which is pure bliss for those pesky bacteria. Dried food doesn't stick to the teeth anywhere near like wet food does. It has more of an abrasive action, providing a helpful hand in oral care. Special dental diets are available, which are a complete diet (so you don't need to feed anything else) but the formation of the biscuit is different, and has the added benefit of certain ingredients to aid oral care. These are good option if your pet likes dried food and is otherwise well. Certain breeds are predisposed to dental problems such as Yorkshire terriers, Poodles and Persians. Specific breed diets are available for these pets which, again is another good option particularly if combined with one of the other methods such as the gel or brushing.

Regular check-ups (at least every 6 months) with your vet or vet nurse should be viewed with same seriousness as ours; if you are unsure of which method is right for your pet, speak to your veterinary surgeon or veterinary nurse, they will be happy to help (we don't give stickers though, sorry!).

The image opposite of Lulu's teeth shows how regular dental care makes a difference. These are teeth of a **12 year old** Labrador, all 42 teeth are present and correct. Cats have a total of 30 teeth in case you wondered.

The numbers are less for the deciduous set of teeth (baby teeth) and these will start to drop out around 4–5 months old and should all have been replaced with the permanent teeth by approximately 7 months old. Ssshhh, the tooth fairy will only deliver pet gifts the following day, if the tooth is placed under their bed before 2pm, otherwise, who knows when she'll have time to come back again! (Bet you didn't know that!)

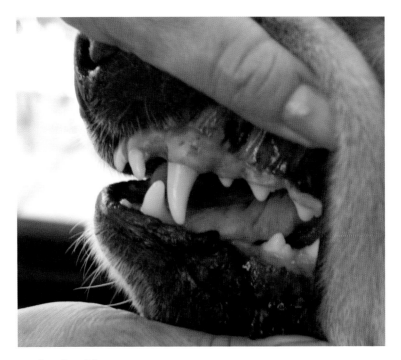

Things to check with your vet

- Smelly breath.
- Any lumps or swelling around the gums, tongue, cheeks and jowls.
- Areas of redness or red spots on the gums.
- Pain on eating – your pet may cry or use other vocal signs when eating. They may paw at their mouth or rub their mouth on the floor or furniture. They may become aggressive towards their food or refuse to eat at all.
- Swellings seen on the outside of the face between the cheek bone and eye.
- Dropping of food from the mouth unintentionally.
- Any bleeding/pus/discharges from the mouth or nose, heavily stained teeth or teeth with large amounts of tartar.
- Any black markings/holes seen on the chewing surface of teeth particularly in dogs.
- Any holes (these can be incredibly small) seen on the front of the enamel particularly in cats.
- Any retained deciduous teeth after 7 months old.
- Moderate to severe gingivitis particularly in young cats, un-vaccinated cats and those who tend to brawl with the other street cats

So there we go, something can be done, we can all now stop asking our pets to leave the room and wishing they wouldn't breathe on us!

Happy brushing and smile!

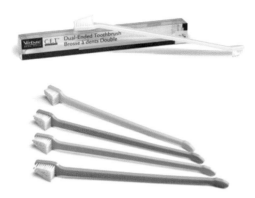

Dual ended toothbrush

Long handle with reverse angle allows for easy application. Tapered end conforms to pet's mouth and teeth. Dual-ended for large and small tooth surfaces. Soft bristles ensure a gentle, well tolerated application.

Images and text kindly supplied by Virbac Animal Health

Dual-ended toothbrush

Long handle with reverse angle allows for easy application. Tapered end conforms to pet's mouth and teeth. Dual-ended for large and small tooth surfaces. Soft bristles ensure a gentle, well tolerated application.

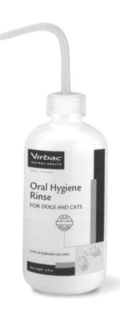

Mouthwash for dogs and cats

Formulated with chlorhexidine gluconate, cetylpyridium chloride and zinc in a soothing alcohol-free vehicle. Helps control levels of bacteria in the mouth without brushing and also freshens breath

Images and text kindly supplied by Virbac Animal Health

Mouthwash for dogs and cats

Formulated with chlorhexidine gluconate, cetylpyridium chloride and zinc in a soothing alcohol-free vehicle. Helps control levels of bacteria in the mouth without brushing and also freshens breath.

Images and text kindly supplied by Virbac Animal Health UK

Botox please!

Botox, fillers, collagen, peels, all-singing all-dancing creams, the list goes on! We spend huge amounts of money and time on this stuff and some of it is pretty good. We always like to look our best, line-free soft skin with that sort after dewy youthful glow – don't we?

Not so for some of our furry friends, in some quarters wrinkles, misshaped features and flat bits are considered the 'must have'. An alien thought to us mere humans, although tempting as it would be far cheaper and less time consuming!

Some breeds, as their breed standard, have wrinkles on their faces, wrinkly bodies or 'flat/squashed' faces. They may have just one of these features or a combination of them. They are bred specifically to include these, the depth and amount of the features does vary. In some, the severity has increased over the years and while they do look cute and adorable, they are not without their problems. It is imperative there is an understanding of these features, how it alters them and how to look after these. Incorrect or lack of maintenance results in an unhappy pet and a lower bank balance for you (and that's no good when the Selfridges' sale is about to start!).

The trouble with being flat

The technical name for flat, squashed faces is brachycephalic, a broad, short shaped skull and these are quite different to the other two shapes of skull: mesocephalic, a more 'normal' shape and doliocephalic, a longer-shaped skull – see image below.

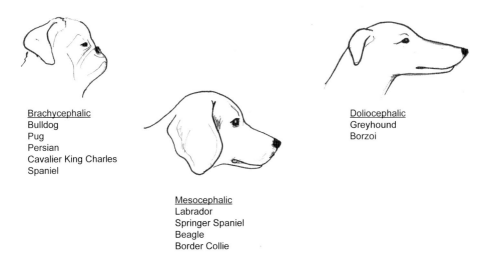

Brachycephalic
Bulldog
Pug
Persian
Cavalier King Charles
Spaniel

Mesocephalic
Labrador
Springer Spaniel
Beagle
Border Collie

Doliocephalic
Greyhound
Borzoi

They all have the same bones and tissues but particularly in the brachycephalic skulls, the layout of them is different compared to those of the other shaped skulls:

Nostrils are narrower

They find it harder to breathe, the nostrils are too narrow to enable enough air in and out in a normal breath. Try breathing through a straw instead of your nose and you will see that size does matter after all! Some will breathe through their mouths (mouth breathing) to get round this problem but it can become dangerously so, in some cases.

The actual nose (muzzle) is narrower and shorter

A short nose and therefore shortened internal nasal cavities, equal the nose looking very flat to the face. In some pets I have seen the nose almost look like two holes in the centre of their faces. This causes the same problems as the narrow nostrils and makes 'normal breathing' even harder.

The tongue is too long

Although you gorgeous ladies might be used to seeing men drool with their tongues hanging out, these pets hang theirs out because it won't fit in their mouths properly! To all the lady doggies though, this doesn't mean your latest flat-faced friend doesn't find you attractive or that they are weird!

The soft palate (towards the back of the mouth) is far too big for their small throats

My mind is awash with humour here and whilst I do sympathise with their problem, I do want this publishing, so here is the sensible version!

The soft palate closes off the nasopharynx while swallowing, so food doesn't enter the respiratory system (please, I'm trying stay focused here!). In these breeds their soft palate is too long, so it obstructs the airway while trying to breathe, causing snoring and snorting. Fantastic – now we have snoring partners and snoring pets – The Dorchester anyone?!

They can also reverse sneeze which I will talk about later, this is slightly different and not so much as a concern as the snoring.

The trachea (windpipe) is narrower

Again, further resistance to breathing as the diameter is too small. Remember the straw and size issue?

Tonsils can be abnormally large

These can stay enlarged all the time, to the point where the size is large enough for them to meet across the back of the throat. Yet another complication to breathing, leading to retching, noisy breathing, gagging – well you would do this too if you felt like you had two… oh never mind! Moving on…

Prognathism

The relationship between the upper and lower jaws (prognathism) is compromised, commonly resulting in either protrusion of the upper jaw (undershot lower jaw) or protrusion of the lower jaw (overshot lower jaw). This can cause issues with eating – your pet may have difficulty picking food up and once they do manage, they then have to try and chew it. This is also a task for them as some of it gets lost amongst the jowls and folds never to be seen again!

Tear duct abnormalities

They can have malformed tear ducts known as epiphora, causing an overflow of tears onto the face.

These differences are abnormalities but considered normal for these types of pets. However it creates what's known as Brachycephalic airway obstruction syndrome (BAOS).

Overall symptoms (with varying degrees of severity) are:

- Difficulty in breathing
- Mouth breathing
- Noisy breathing
- Snoring
- Snorting
- Gagging
- Retching
- Bluish/purple tinge to the tongue and gums due to a lack of oxygen
- Lack of energy
- Exercise and/or heat intolerance
- Syncope (fainting)

How to help

- Keep them out of heat and humidity and don't over exercise – they really can't stand this (totally with them on the exercise part!). Dogs and cats don't sweat; well, a little from the pads but their main way of cooling themselves is by breathing or panting. They already have difficulty breathing normally, so breathing faster and harder to keep cool results in them overheating, their tongue and gums may look blue due to the lack of oxygen and they may even faint. If they do become hyperthermic (too hot) or faint see 'Call 999' chapter for what to do, but they must see a vet.

- Walk them during the cooler periods of the day.

- Gentle exercise, no long runs.

- Keep them at an ideal weight, obesity exacerbates the breathing difficulties.

- If outside in the summer, provide lots of shade – children's paddling pools with cool water in are excellent for them (great excuse for purchasing new garden furniture).

- Provide cool wet towels to sit on if needed.

- Keep the nose, nostrils and eyes clean and free from mucous and dirt.

- Use a harness instead of collar for walking.

- If they are snoring while sleeping, extend their necks or try moving them into a different position to see if that helps.

- If they start snoring when normally they don't, take them to the vet – they could have a inhaled a foreign body into their airways, the dog, not the other half (I've no idea what you do with them!).

Please do not think that the noisy breathing and snoring is 'just the way these breeds breathe', it means they are having problems. Follow the advice above and see your vet.

Reverse sneezing (backwards sneeze)

This isn't actually sneezing but due to an irritation on the soft palate e.g. dusts. Commonly it's the brachycephalic breeds affected, more so the smaller ones but it can occur in any size. They will extend their heads and necks and make repeated gagging/coughing noises when breathing in, concentrate please! (But at least there's a technical name for it!) Whilst this might look concerning it is nothing to worry about, unlike snoring which can become life threatening.

You can just wait for the episode to pass, some methods that have been noted to help the episode pass quicker are: gently blowing in their face, pinching their nose and scratching the throat. These episodes can happen at any random point although it is common during sleep or just after they have woken up (or whenever they feel the need to embarrass you).

Keeping the wrinkles (well if you insist!)

Examples of dogs with wrinkles:

> Shar Pei
> Pug
> Bulldog
> Dogue de Bordeaux
> Neapolitan Mastiff

The following regime has to be taken in to account when taking on one of these dogs. Wrinkles on the face and body need specific care to prevent sores, itchy skin and infections in between the folds – skin fold dermatitis (this is a form of surface Pyoderma).

Beauty regime for wrinklies!

- Check weekly to ensure there is no redness or smell coming from in between the folds.

- Clean with warm water every couple of days. Wipe in between each fold and wrinkle with a clean soft cloth, cotton buds may also be used (just not down the ears) – the dirt in there is what starts to smell and boy they can whiff!

- After wiping clean they must be dried. If they are left damp, they will become red and sore and bacterial growth leading to infection is encouraged.

- Brush weekly, particularly if they are shedding a lot, as the loose hair irritates the skin in between the folds.

- Regular baths will help keep them in tip top condition. Usually every 6–8 weeks, overdoing it can cause more problems.

- Keep feet dry, dry off with a towel or hair dryer after walks.
- Keep nails short, overly long nails will encourage them to chew their feet. If they have long fur in between their pads this needs to be kept short as well. Long fur and knots in their feet will also encourage chewing.
- If the smell changes or becomes worse this can be a sign of infection and you need to see your vet.
- Other signs of infection are redness, sores, bald patches, irritation and itching. To itch their wrinkles and folds, they will rub their faces or the relevant part of their bodies on objects or on the floor (a nightmare if you have cream carpets).

Decubitus Ulcers

These are areas of thickened skin over bony prominences, usually the elbows and hocks. They can look red and ulcerated and sometimes bleed. There are very common in older pets and thin dogs such as Greyhounds. Your vet will need to take a look at them if they are inflamed, bleeding or oozing, otherwise keep them clean and dry and provide lots of soft bedding for them to lie on. Padded bedding should be provided for these types of pets, regardless if ulcers are present or not. The pressure of lying on hard surfaces increases the development of these, much like pressure sores in humans.

Can't find the itch

Skin diseases and all their associated problems are unfortunately notoriously difficult to treat, as the cause of these things is a minefield. They can arise from parasites, bacteria, fungus, allergies, and food intolerances to name a few. Below are some of the common skin diseases that I get asked about, numerous times a week. Your vet must always be seen regarding skin problems or suspicious skin – some breeds are prone to skin conditions, Westies being a common one as are the wrinkly pets already mentioned.

Signs of skin disease

Below are the technical names of the symptoms and a brief description, as often these terms are used but not always understood:

Alopecia – loss of hair.

Lesions – sore areas of various sizes often red, inflamed and may weep (this description also sounds a little like me when I'm enraged!).

Dermatitis – inflammation of the skin.

Erosions – ulcerated areas of skin.

Erythema – red skin caused by inflammation (like a bad reaction to fake tan or the £100 face cream, which you now wish you'd never bought!).

Lichenification – thickening of the superficial layers of skin.

Pruritus – intense and persistent itching (the return of the bad fake tan reaction!).

Pustules – small pus-filled lesion.

These signs can be seen in varying degrees of severity and there is usually a combination of a few.

Parasitic skin disease

Disease caused by parasites such as fleas, Sarcoptes (scabies), Demodex, lice, Otodectes (ear mites), these produce some of the above signs of skin disease but the parasite or mite needs to be identified and treated before the skin disease will cease. More information on some of these irritating creatures can be found in the 'Creepy Crawlies' chapter.

Malassezia Pachydermitis

Malassezia must be one of the most common skin conditions I hear being bandied about. But do you really understand what it is?

Malassezia Pachydermitis by its formal name is yeast found on the skin of healthy animals and doesn't normally cause any problems. Should the skin environment change, example due to a skin allergy, then Malassezia yeast can turn into a pathogen i.e. will cause disease. It will produce red, itchy, scaly, greasy skin, some bald or thin patches of hair, with thickening of the skin and ear infections (Otitis Externa) in some cases. Typically the areas affected are under the chin and neck, between the toes, armpit and groin areas. Your vet can diagnose this by looking at a sample of the hair and skin under the microscope that is stained with dye, you don't have a choice of colours, I'm afraid! For extra 'I'm brainy' points at the pub quiz Malassezia looks like blue milk bottles (not sure which pub quiz would include that question but you never know!).

You will more than likely be given a shampoo and perhaps other medication too. The symptoms from Malassezia will just continue to repeat though, if the underlying cause is not addressed and treated.

Allergic skin disease

There are different types of allergies that cause skin disease. To get an accurate diagnosis of which allergen is causing the problem, your vet may recommend various tests which may include blood tests, microscopy examination of the skin and Intradermal skin testing (various allergens are injected into a patch of skin and their reactions monitored). Once the allergen is identified it may be treated by simply removing it, changing the diet or special vaccines can be made to name some of the treatments.

Types of allergic skin disease include:

Flea allergic dermatitis – the pet is allergic to the saliva from the flea's bite, causing very itchy red skin. The itching often leads to self-trauma and these wounds (lesions) usually become infected with bacteria or Malassezia. Treatments may include prescription flea treatments, antibiotics, steroids or antihistamines. Extra essential fatty acids are also helpful. If your pet is prone to this allergy you should use preventative flea and worm treatment consistently throughout the year.

Atopy (atopic dermatitis) – the pet is allergic to environmental allergens such as dust mites and pollens. Some breeds are predisposed to this, such as Westies, German Shepherds, Shar Peis, Boxers and many more! Similar signs to flea allergy are produced, i.e. itchy, red skin but also it tends to be greasy and there can be bald patches with thickening of the skin. Again bacteria and Malassezia often infect these skins as a secondary problem. The allergen needs diagnosing and treatment, secondary bacterial or Malassezia should be treated as well.

Hives (Urticaria), contact dermatitis and intolerances/hypersensitivity to food are other types of allergic skin disease.

Seborrhoea – A common disorder of the skin where there is an abnormality in the sebum production and can appear in 3 forms:

1. Seborrhoea Oleosa – caused by an excess of sebum creating greasy and oily skin, they find this irritating and itchy. There may well be stinky with this one!

2. Seborrhoea sicca – caused by an excess of skin cells. Too many skin cells are produced which shed, leaving dandruff. Usually there is lots of the snow stuff along with dry, itchy skin. Do not use human anti-dandruff shampoo.

3. Seborrhoea dermatitis – this is either the greasy or dry version which has become inflamed.

There are lots of causes of seborrhoea and various treatments. If your pet is prone to one of these conditions, then bathing them in a veterinary dermatology shampoos which is appropriate to the signs your pet is showing, can help maintain healthy skin and hair.

Pyoderma – Another skin disease caused by bacteria, which is usually secondary to another disease. Pyoderma has varying depths:

Surface e.g. acute moist dermatitis, skin fold dermatitis.

Superficial e.g. Impetigo.

Deep e.g. Interdigital (in between toes), Furunculosis.

Describing the symptoms of each of these, where they occur and treatments will start to verge on boring you to tears. Go and see your vet who can decide on its depth and treatment. At least if they mention any of these words you will have a vague idea what they are on about! These are more common in dogs than cats by the way.

Ringworm (Dermatophytosis)

This IS NOT a worm! It's a fungal disease. More common in cats than in dogs and it is passed by direct contact and indirect contact e.g. via bowls and other objects (no sharing).

Remember with this one, it is zoonotic, which means we can get it from them – aarrgh! Take it from me, these round red raised sore patches, which can affect the skin, hair and nail beds is not a good look! Your vet can sort your pet out but you will have to see your doctor and no, the doctor can't treat your pet as a freebie!

Beauty regime for the itchies

- See your vet if you spot any of the signs mentioned in this chapter, skin is a very broad subject and signs can be vague to severe.

- Keep feet dry, dry off with a towel or hair dryer after walks, you may need to rinse these first with water to remove any outside allergens.

- Keep nails short, overly long nails will encourage them to chew their feet. If they have long fur in between their pads this needs to be kept short as well. Long fur and knots in their feet will also encourage chewing.

- Use preventative flea and worm treatment all year round.

- Prevent itching – when a pet itches, histamines are released which then make the skin itchy again, the pet scratches, histamines are released and so the vicious circle continues. Stopping them itching is part of the key to getting on top of skin disease. See Appendix 3 on 'how to prevent self-interference'.

- If your pet is given a special diet or a food elimination programme make sure you stick to this. No treats or cheating, if you don't stick it to properly you will be wasting your time and money and not helping your pet's skin situation.

- If your pet is prescribed mediation, make sure it's given consistently.

- Bathing your pet that has skin disease is a good idea but always be guided by your vet. There are veterinary dermatology shampoos which help most of the skin issues and it is definitely advisable to use these, rather than a shampoo blended from handpicked berries, infused with green tea and freshly caught seaweed. Don't go wasting your Chanel No 5 or Miss Dior on them either!

Your next appointment, darling, is…

Virbac Animal Health UK and the Feline Advisory Bureau, are a good sources of information on skin (see Useful Contacts).

Creepy crawlies

Boys may like looking at bugs and wanting unmentionables in their bedrooms but we certainly don't. We already race around (stylishly of course) running the house, children, pets, work, sorting the food shop that magically appears. Foot down, no juggling of the bugs as well and the money you saved on the BOGOFF offer on toilet rolls at the supermarket (does everyone fall for this one or is it just me?) can pay for the treatment that works and keeps the blighters away!

There are lots and lots of creepy crawlies that affect our pets, these are known as parasites. A parasite by definition is an organism which lives on or within another animal. The parasite obtains its nutrition from that animal, often the parasite lives at the expense of and causes harm to the animal.

Parasites affect our pets on both the inside of their bodies (endoparasites) and on the outsides of their bodies (ectoparasites). They use your pets like we use hotels and restaurants, I wonder if parasites grade the service too?

Let's work from the inside out and look at the internal parasites first. There are some funny sounding names in this chapter and it doesn't matter if you can't pronounce them. The information is there to increase your knowledge, so you can make good judgement when looking at products or treatments to use on your pet. There are many treatments on the market for all the different bugs but be warned, they are not all the same. Better to buy one product once that works, rather than buying various ones that don't and in the end, costing you a lot more. Use the universal shopping rule – know what you want before you go and buy!

Some of the internal parasites live in the intestines (gastrointestinal worms) and some live in other areas of the body such as the lungs. Wherever they are and whatever they are we do not want them!

Another few potential *zzzzzz* moments but feel free to squirm away!

Nematodes (roundworms)

Toxocara
There are three types of Toxocara worm: Toxocara Canis (affects dogs and foxes), Toxocara Cati (affects cats) and Toxocara Leonina (affects dogs, cats and foxes).

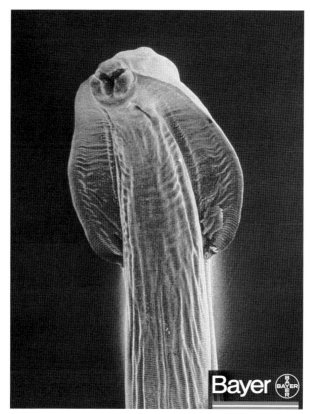

Image kindly supplied by Bayer

Toxocara Canis – In real life they look like spaghetti and can be up to 10cm long, apologies if you are about to delve into your tomato and olive angel hair pasta! They do live in the intestines but its conduct varies depending on the age of the dog. It is during the larvae stage that this worm is infective (the larva is the name given to the part of the lifecycle between an egg and an adult).

In puppies under 12 weeks old, these larvae migrate from the intestines and end up in the lungs, they are then coughed up and swallowed, returning back to the intestines. Infestations in puppies can result in a pot-bellied appearance, diarrhoea, vomiting (don't be surprised if it looks like wriggling spaghetti!) and weight loss. Heavy infestations can cause blockage of the intestines, which will require emergency treatment.

In older dogs the larvae still migrate but tend to fail to reach the lungs and will settle in the muscle, brain, kidneys, heart and liver. Here they remain dormant (producing no clinical signs) until such a time they are stimulated, a very common stimulus is pregnancy.

Around day 42 of pregnancy in the bitch, the larvae become activated and pass across the placenta into the foetuses, some also travel to the mammary glands and infect the puppies when they initially feed. Most puppies are born infected with Toxocara Canis.

Toxocara Canis has the ability to infect humans and cause disease (i.e. it is zoonotic). I realise you won't eat these for a laugh but it is easy to consume the eggs and larvae unknowingly.

The eggs are passed in the faeces of dogs and foxes and cannot be seen with the naked eye. If a dog has shed eggs, they can easily end up on our hands. This is particularly so with children in areas like playgrounds (OK and us – admit it, we like to go on the swings and those spring rocking things too, he he!). Anyway, children are always putting their hands in their mouths and adults too – how many of you bite your nails or don't wash your hands after preparing the rib eye steak? There you go, that's all it takes and boom, they're in! Toxocara Canis can cause what is known as 'visceral larval margins' as the eggs migrate to one of our organs and cause illness. If the larvae migrate to the eye then this can potentially cause blindness.

Toxocara Cati and ***Leonina*** are similar to Toxocara Canis. Cati is not however passed via the placenta, only via the milk. It is not known if it is zoonotic. Toxocara Leonina is general seen in older dogs and cats, as it is not passed through the placenta or via the milk.

Other nematodes or roundworms include hookworm, whipworm and lungworm. One lungworm in particular – Angiostrongylus Vasorum – is becoming more topical as it is spread by snails and slugs. The ingestion of frogs can also infect the dog, obviously dogs must see these creatures as a delicacy too! Foxes, badgers and ferrets can be infected with this particular lungworm but not cats. Again it is part of the larvae stage that is infective and they migrate to the heart and to the lung arteries. Here they are coughed up, swallowed and travel down to the intestines, to be then passed out in the faeces. This worm causes symptoms such as coughing, difficulty in breathing, not eating, bleeding abnormalities and pneumonia. In heavy burdens heart failure and sudden death can occur. The problems and symptoms associated with this worm are being seen to be on the increase in the UK.

Cestodes (tapeworms)

The tapeworms affecting the dog and cat are Dipylidium caninum (affects dogs and cats), Echinococcus granulosus (affects dogs) and the Taenia species (affects dogs and cats).

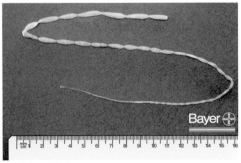

Image kindly supplied by Bayer

Tapeworms live in the intestines as one long worm made up of small segments. As the worm matures, segments break off and are excreted in the faeces. These can be seen around the anus as small white mobile segments, much like grains of rice. Again, apologies if you are about to tuck into your seafood risotto!

Dipylidium caninum

Probably the most common tapeworm in the UK, it lives in the small intestine and the full chain or worm can be up to 50cm long. It does not often cause disease unless there is a heavy infestation. It is however transmitted by fleas and lice. The excreted segments shed eggs, which are eaten by the flea. These eggs then start to develop into the tapeworm whilst in the flea. If the dog or cat ingests the flea or louse, (very common when grooming themselves) the developing tapeworm within the flea, continues to develop in the intestines of the dog or cat. Sometimes dogs may feel itchy around their bottom (anal pruritus) more often, though itchy bottoms are a sign that anal glands need emptying.

The control of fleas and lice is key in helping to control this tapeworm.

Echinococcus granulosus

This tapeworm is approximately 6cm long and can affect dogs. It sheds its segments roughly once a week. This tapeworm is zoonotic and a particular health concern as it causes hydatid disease in humans. The cysts can develop in the liver, brain, lungs or bones and it is possible for the cyst to grow to the size of a football in humans, if left untreated it can become potentially fatal.

Dogs should not be allowed to consume carcasses, uncooked meat or raw offal in the aid of controlling this tapeworm.

Taenia species

Unless there is a heavy infestation this tapeworm rarely causes disease. There are many types of the Taenia tapeworm with their eggs being passed in faeces and are common in farm areas as they tend to be spread across large areas of land.

Again, prevention is aided by not allowing your dog to consume carcasses, uncooked meat or raw offal, not that you would find these in any of our sophisticated fridges but just in case you were thinking about it, don't.

Protozoal Parasites

Because of the health risk I feel Toxoplasmosis gondii and Giardia, by their formal names, need a mention.

These are another type of parasite known as protozoa.

Toxoplasmosis can be transmitted by any warm-blooded animal but ends its journey in the cat. The eggs or oocysts are passed in faeces and these have the potential to cause cysts in humans. The cysts are teeny tiny and can cause illness and flu-like symptoms but otherwise do not create any problems unless it is:

1. A pregnant woman. Toxoplasmosis can cause abortion, stillbirth and foetal abnormalities (sheep should also be avoided).

2. Anyone who is immunosuppressed e.g. babies, the elderly, those suffering with HIV-infection or those receiving chemotherapy treatment.

If you fall into these categories extra precautions are needed. You don't need to re-home your beloved cat, just be sensible. There are some tips below, but any concerns should be brought to the attention of your doctor, midwife or nurse immediately. There is a blood test available to check if you have been exposed to this protozoa.

1. Avoid emptying and cleaning litter trays if you can. If you have to do this, wear gloves and wash hands thoroughly afterwards.

2. Wash your hands after handling or grooming your cat.

3. Keep away and refrain from handling sheep.

4. Cats like to bury their poo. If you are a keen gardener wear gloves, as you are likely to come across the delightful stuff while planting your geraniums.

5. Ensure meat is thoroughly cooked.

6. Wash your hands after handling raw meat

Giardia is one of the common causes of diarrhoea in humans. Again this is passed to humans by consuming the cysts passed by faeces. It can also cause death in cage birds such as budgies.

Treating and controlling the worms

All dogs and cats should be treated regularly and is part of responsible ownership. Unless their faeces is examined under the microscope for worm eggs, you will not know if they have worms. Waiting until you 'see them' is not the way to keep pets healthy – think of all the pets and people that will have become infected and the illnesses caused if you adopt this approach.

The current guidelines are taken from the European Scientific Counsel Companion Animal Parasites (ESCCAP) – very lovely and clever people!

Puppies

Puppies are likely to be born with Toxocara or become infected from the bitch's milk at a very young age. Worm treatment needs to begin at 2 weeks old and repeated every 2 weeks thereafter until they are fully weaned, treatment is then reduced to monthly intervals until they are 6 months old.

Kittens

Kittens are not born with Toxocara but can become infected from the queen's milk. Worm treatment needs to begin at 3 weeks old and repeated every fortnight until 2 weeks after weaning, treatment is then reduced to monthly intervals until they are 6 months old.

<u>Dogs and cats over 6 months old</u>
Treatment for both roundworm and tapeworm is required every 3 months equating to 4 times a year. In cases of high risk such boarding kennels or households with children, treatment for roundworm can be given monthly.

<u>Pregnant and nursing bitches and queens</u>
Pregnant bitches should be treated daily from approximately day 42 of pregnancy, until the puppies are born. A further treatment should be given with the first treatment of the puppies.

Pregnant queens need only be treated at the same time as the kitten's first treatment.

Other methods of control

1. PICK UP THE POO AND BIN IT– do not dispose of it in compost or flush it down the toilet. There are some very stylish poo bags now, with a range of patterns and colours – beats the nappy bag!
2. Use flea treatment regularly to prevent the spread of the tapeworm Dipylidium caninum.
3. Wash your hands after handling pets and raw meat. Children especially should wash their hands following playing in an area where dogs are likely to have been e.g. the park.
4. Children's play areas should be fenced off to prevent the entry of animals.
5. Keep sandboxes covered and change the sand regularly.
6. Local councils are responsible for enforcing the laws regarding dog fouling.

Are you ready for more? Of course you are, this time, get ready to itch!

Ectoparasites live on the outside on the body, some can be seen with the naked eye and some can't. The most common one of these are fleas, so they seem like a good one to begin with!

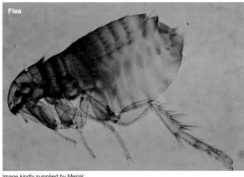

Flea

Image kindly supplied by Merial

Ctenocephalides (fleas)

There are three types of flea – the cat flea (which is the most common flea on cats and dogs), the dog flea (uncommon and only affects dogs) and the human flea (yes, a human one! Thankfully these are now rare in the UK). The cat flea however will bite humans.

Fleas are wingless insects and their favourite meal is blood, that's the only thing they need and want (bet that isn't on Jamie Oliver's menu!).

The easiest way to understand fleas is to understand their lifecycle. 95% of the flea population is in the environment, that means your carpets, lovely cushions, their bed, your bed (this can become embarrassing and I do have a few tales but I shall refrain from divulging, not about me I hasten to add!); only 5% of the population is on your pet.

Fleas are itchy and cause distress to pets, there is the problem flea allergic dermatitis as well, as outlined in 'Botox please!'. Flea bites on humans look like small red lumps that you could scratch until they bleed. They are very common around the ankles, as fleas can jump to approximately this height from the ground.

The life cycle of the flea

The whole life cycle takes between 3 and 4 weeks but may be quicker in warmer weather.

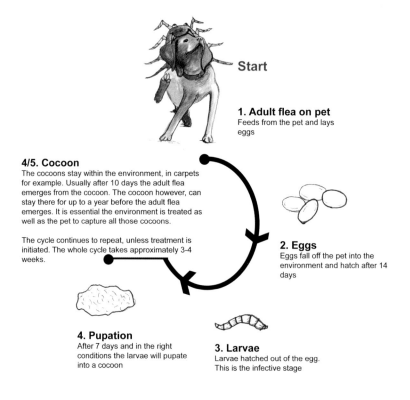

Start

1. Adult flea on pet
Feeds from the pet and lays eggs

4/5. Cocoon
The cocoons stay within the environment, in carpets for example. Usually after 10 days the adult flea emerges from the cocoon. The cocoon however, can stay there for up to a year before the adult flea emerges. It is essential that the environment is treated as well as the pet to capture all those cocoons.

The cycle continues to repeat, unless treatment is initiated. The whole cycle takes approximately 3-4 weeks.

2. Eggs
Eggs fall off the pet into the environment and hatch after 14 days

4. Pupation
After 7 days and in the right conditions the larvae will pupate into a cocoon

3. Larvae
Larvae hatched out of the egg. This is the infective stage

As they feed on lots of blood, it goes without saying they poo lots of blood. Flea dirt is often seen before adult fleas and looks like small black specks within their coat. Your vet or vet nurse will be able to check if this is flea dirt or just everyday dirt.

If fleas have become an issue, deal with it immediately, do not put it on the 'to do' list.

Treat your pets with a suitable product that is proven to work, all cats and dogs in the household must be done. Don't justify wanting to pay less money with reasons like 'I've only seen them on the cat not the dog'. They probably are on the dog you just haven't seen them, as they do hop on and off.

Your house or environment absolutely must be treated, otherwise the fleas will continue to hatch out and jump on your pct. Although your pet may have been treated and this will kill any fleas that jump on them, there will be hundreds more behind them – ready to leap out from behind the futon!

Spraying the environment with a proven treatment will see to all the little critters hiding in your house. If you don't spray the environment you're going to potentially have a constant flea problem. The best way to avoid all this is to use flea treatment preventatively all year round. It used to be thought that fleas were a summer problem, mainly because it is warmer (which fleas like), but factors such as central heating, lots of vibration (people movement), carbon dioxide (from breathing) amongst others also appeal to fleas – this will explain a sudden appearance by them if you have just moved into a new house for example. Fleas in modern day life are now a year-round drama not just a summer one. Don't let them become the latest episode in your life!

Linognathus setosus and Trichodectes canis and Felicola subrostratus (lice)

Lots and lots of big words that all mean the very small word – lice! There are three types of lice, Linognathus (the sucking louse) and Trichodectes (the biting louse) and Felicola subrostratus (a cat biting louse). They are transmitted by close contact or by items such as combs and brushes although, unlike fleas, they cannot survive for long away from the animal or on different animals. Lice are host specific e.g. the cat louse can only survive on cats, not on other animals; again fleas can survive on a few different animals as they are not host specific.

Like fleas these are small wingless insects. The biting louse feeds on scales, feathers, scabs and loose skin cells (another one for Jamie Oliver's menu!). The sucking louse feeds on blood and tissue fluids. An infestation of lice is called pediculosis and severe cases of this are often associated with neglect. They cause severe itching and in doing so, your pet can cause trauma to themselves as well, making the skin sore and open to infection.

The eggs of lice stick onto the hair and these are tiny but can be seen with the naked eye but only just. These are the pet's version of nits (nits are the eggs of lice). Whilst our teachers might have frogmarched us off to the nit nurse and our parents washed our hair in vinegar and combed it with one of those awful combs, incredibly painful if you have very thick hair like me I'd like to add (Mother!). Our pets need a treatment proven to work, that does the job, simply as that. A lot of these are in the 'spot on' formulas, which usually treat fleas and ticks as well – fantastic!

Use these regularly all year round to prevent them coming in the first place.

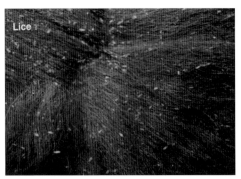

Image kindly supplied by Merial

Ixodes (ticks)

Ticks are arachnids, they posses eight legs (like spiders); insects like the fleas and ticks mentioned, have only six legs. These too are wingless and spend most of the time away from your pet, only jumping on board to feed. Keeping in line with the common theme here, they too use blood as their food. To feed, a tick will sink its mouthparts into the pet's skin and secrete a substance which prevents the blood from clotting (they think of everything these days!). There they will stay until full and they decide to fall off. A tick that has just fed looks a small grey pebble.

Image kindly supplied by Merial

When removing a tick, care needs to be taken that the mouthparts aren't left behind in your pet's skin. If you just pull it off, that is likely to happen and commonly they become infected.

Use special tools available to 'lift' them out or place a piece of cotton wool soaked in tick treatment and, once dead, it can be gently removed. Smearing them in margarine or butter can work as the tick starts to lose its grip and falls off.

Ticks are very common in areas with lots of heather or greenery. These, like fleas and lice, are preventable by using proven treatments.

If you're unsure which products and treatments are worthy of your pet and your cash, vets or vet nurses will happily discuss it with you, as there are few different ones. They don't all last the same amount of time and they may treat a range of things. Let's keep these everyday bugs out of our lives, we have enough to deal with, without these!

Night, night don't let the bedbugs bite!

Help, I'm having a bad hair day!

Before we start wanting the latest cute cut from the pet hair styles weekly and adding the styling gel and glitter, what is the point of skin and hair anyway? Do we need to bother with it the same as we would our own? And if they won't let you anywhere near them with a brush what are you meant to do?

Back to the basics!

The term integument refers to skin, hair, feathers, nails and claws, whatever is covering the body. Hopefully our bodies aren't covered in feathers but covered with gorgeous to-die-for skin. Scented oils and chocolate sauce are not part of the integument but certainly make it a lot more fun!

Skin and nails

The point of skin is to:

Provide protection – against bugs, chemicals, harmful UV rays.

Regulate body temperature – an example of this is when it is too cold (I'm not going where you think I am with this one!).

Hair will stand up on end to trap any heat beneath, helping to maintain and increase body temperature.

Store nutrients.

Produce vitamin D.

Allow communication via excretions e.g. pheromones.

Allow sensory perception of the environment.

Skin is split into essentially three layers: the Epidermis – the surface and probably what we all think of as skin – varies in thickness from very thin to extremely thick e.g. their pads and noses. It is impervious i.e. waterproof and does not contain any blood vessels. The Dermis is the next layer – this houses all the bits like blood vessels, sweat glands, sebaceous glands, hair follicles and nerve endings. The bottom layer is the Hypodermis and generally consists of tissues and fat.

Pads and noses

The epidermis part of the pads is very thick and has no hair, the dermis part is also thickened and contains lots of blood vessels and fat. The pads of dogs and cats are their version of shock absorbers and provide the cushioned support needed for running and jumping, (due to the lack of 'pads' on my own feet I feel this is excellent justification for NEVER running!).

Noses are made up in the same way and have their own unique pattern, just like our fingertips. So when the Sunday roast or the Belgian chocolates have gone missing, whip out that silver powdery stuff to find out which nose or fingers it was! I don't know where you get the silver powdery stuff though, so maybe there is a big flaw in my detective work!

Pads and noses are the only part of dogs' and cats' bodies that sweat. To clear up a myth I hear all the time, a warm nose does not mean they are poorly, nor does a cold wet nose mean they are well.

Nails

The nails are a special form of epidermis and contain a substance called keratin which makes these tougher and harder. They do contain a dermis and it is this part that contains the blood vessels (the quick, as it is commonly known), which causes the nails to bleed if they are cut too far back. The nails grow in two sheets and have a groove underneath.

Cats' nails stay retracted by special muscles and ligaments around the nail; these also allow the cat to extend and retract them when needed – I have known some people with this ability, doesn't quite work the same though!

Hair

I often wonder if we all shaved our hair off would we still look as attractive, or is our hair and its style one of the most defining features we have? I think it is and considering the amount of time we spend making sure it looks good (and the cash) it should be one of our most defining features!

Hair is something that can make us feel like a million dollars but if it's not right, oh dear me, the whole day can be black! Some men may not bat an eyelid if we have a new fantastic hair cut but they sure as hell notice if we don't bother with our luscious locks! Having itchy, knotty manky looking hair is no fun away.

Dogs and cats have amazing hair, look at all the different shapes, the colours, textures and the styles – as their owner you are responsible for keeping it like that. Knotted and unkempt hair doesn't make our dogs and cats feel great either. Come on, you don't want 'the look' from people that your dog or cat's hair is appalling; comments like 'he looks stunning', or 'where do you get her hair done' are far better and further credit to you that you have an amazing looking pet, as well as everything else you do!

Here's the brain behind the hair!

You will remember the different layers of skin (go and re-read if you have to!). Hair starts its formation in the epidermis layer and grows down into the dermis layer where it forms a hair cone. The hair then begins growing back up from the hair cone, the epidermis cells above it are destroyed leaving a clear space called the hair follicle. Hair grows through the hair follicle, eventually dies and breaks off from the hair cone. After this, the hair will shed out, or it may stay within the hair supported by other hairs until it is groomed out. A new hair will start to grow alongside the dead one before it is lost. This cycle happens in all dogs and cats; hair in our pets does not continually grow but works in this cycle, the hair follicles are all at different points of the cycle at different times – hence why we don't see bald pets (they don't seem to suffer with receding or thinning issues either!).

This does means however, ALL PETS MOULT, the myth that certain breeds such as Poodles, Schnauzers and too many others to mention do not lose their hair is simply not true. The hair of all breeds of dogs and cats follow this cycle.

Moulting is shedding of the hair and technically this is seasonal – dogs would normally shed in the spring and autumn, cats normally shed mostly in the spring and less so through the summer and autumn. The rate, speed or amount of shedding is dependent on factors such as temperature, sunlight, breed, age, hormones and nutrition. Our lovely centrally-heated homes though, are a predominant factor in why moulting or shedding can be a year round issue. When the hairs end up on that LBD however, something has to be done!

All pets have three different types of hair:

Guard hairs or **primary hairs** – These are the longer and stiffer and make up the topcoat. Guard hairs provide the waterproof layer of the coat.

Wool hairs or **secondary hairs** – These are shorter and much softer and make up the undercoat.

Vibrissae or **tactile hairs**, otherwise known as the whiskers – These are very thick and are much longer than the rest of the coat. They grow from follicles within the hypodermis, rather than the dermis. Whiskers are mainly found on the upper lip, above the eyes, on the cheek (dogs only) and behind the carpus or wrist (cats only). These tactile hairs are so called because they are used as a sensory tool; nerve endings in the bottom of the whiskers respond to hair movement and also help a pet judge the width of spaces. These should never be cut.

The amount of primary and secondary hairs differs for each breed, hence all the different types of coats.

Sebaceous glands

Each hair follicle has a gland called the sebaceous gland. It sits on the side of the follicle and secretes sebum onto the growing hair. Sebum is important, it is this stuff that creates the waterproofness of the hair, plays a role in territorial marking and produces pheromones which help attract the opposite sex – this is what we need girlies, bottles of sebum not serum! It does have a downside though, that wet dog smell we hate is due to sebum and it can cause greasy or dry skin – explained more in the chapter 'Botox please!'

Anal glands

These are two sacs located just underneath the anus and are a special form of sebaceous gland. Each time the pet defecates, a small amount is squeezed onto the surface of the faeces. It is a territorial marker and why dogs in particulary, smell other faeces. Anal sac secretion absolutely honks! Full anal glands (i.e. they haven't being emptying themselves) are a very common problem in the dog. This can be due to recent bouts of diarrhoea, low fibre diets or narrow ducts. They may display the following symptoms:

A foul smell.

Licking at their bottom.

Scooting along the floor – this is not usually a sign of worms but their anal glands being full.

Straining when passing faeces.

Inflammation and abscess can occur.

It is best to let the professionals empty these (lucky us!) and if they having repeated problems they may require further treatment such as flushing the sacs, your vet will advise on the right course of action for your pet.

Baby hair

There is truth behind this saying. Puppies and kittens are not born with smooth peachy skin. They are however, born with lots of secondary hairs and no primary ones. This gives them the soft fluffy hair often referred to as puppy hair. Between the ages of 6–8 months a good stock of primary hair has grown, changing the look of the hair to what I often hear being called their 'adult fur'. Colour changes and markings may continue up until this point. You can't take it back for a refund or exchange it, if it turns out to be a different colour or pattern than what you wanted.

Hairdressers and beauticians

I love going to both of these places I don't always get as often as I would like to, mainly due to a lack of time but I still go. As, like the rest of the human race, my hair has to be cut and although my nails don't HAVE to be painted, nor is a facial essential, they make such a difference to our look and more importantly our wellbeing and state of mind, that I am therefore declaring all of these essential!

Whilst dogs and cats might not appreciate being sat at the nail bar with a glass of champagne, they do appreciate having their hair and other bits sorted. The same reasons apply, yes they need grooming and other treatments to stop knots forming or to prevent the fleas invading for example but it makes them feel better as well. I love looking after old pets, a bath and blow dry with a good massage might sound daft but to an old pet that may have arthritic joints and muscle wastage this is pure heaven and the difference in these dogs and cats when they go home is very evident.

Keeping the skin peachy perfect

Although we don't visibly see their skin as much as ours, most of the same principles apply. Feed a good complete diet that is right for your pet's age, breed and lifestyle – see chapter 'For the main course I would like…' for more help on this. I cannot express enough, the difference a good quality diet makes to their skin and hair. Access to water is mandatory; they don't have a 2 litre a day rule! Looking after their hair is also key in maintaining their skin condition.

Dogs and cats with white or pale coloured ears and noses should have sunscreen applied to them daily, to protect them against the harmful UV rays. Obviously this is more relevant in the summer or whenever the UK decides to grace us with a sunny day. These types are particularly prone to sunburn and to developing skin cancers. A high factor such as SPF 30 should be used; although human sunscreens have been used up to press, a dedicated pet sunscreen has now being developed.

Use preventative flea, lice and tick treatments regularly. Any odd looking marks, lumps, whiffs or scratching should be brought to your vet's attention.

They don't need exfoliating, microdermabrasion or tinted moisturisers.

To the salon or not to the salon

There are many different treatments and options for your pet at the salon, at least there is at Fuchsia's health spa. If you struggle to care for their hair at home, either due to time or your pet hates you going anywhere near with a comb, make life easier for yourself and take them to the professionals. Far better to do this regularly than leaving it until they are in a smelly matted state, as often you may not end up with the cut you wanted and a larger bill.

The most common requirement is a full groom. This is what should be included in a full groom at the very least:

Bath in an appropriate shampoo and conditioner if required (not all coats require conditioner).

Blow dry, removing any knots at the same time.

Trimming work, should include the body, face, tail, legs, ears and feet – this may be with scissors and/or clippers.

Anal glands emptied.

Eyes cleaned.

Ears cleaned and plucked.

Nails cut.

For most dogs, this is required every 6–8 weeks. Poodles and Bichon Frise are slightly different because of their very curly coats and should have a full groom every 4 weeks.

Each breed has its own breed standard hair cut or show cut. Whether you choose to keep the traditional look or choose a different one is entirely your choice, just make sure it is a style you can cope with, much like being able 'to do' your own hair. There are many books, guides and websites which cover all the breeds, their hair types and relevant styles. To discuss each breed type and its hair is far beyond what this chapter is about, but check in the useful contacts as I will list some useful sources of information.

Nails and ears – can be overlooked, a good groomer though will check these each time without fail.

Ears that are not regularly cleaned and/or plucked will continue to fill up with hair and wax. Not only does this interfere with hearing, it's uncomfortable and they are far more likely to get ear infections – See chapter 'Ears what it's about', on how to spot ear infections and look after their ears. Ear cleaning and plucking is something most salons or vets can do, if you prefer not to.

Nails, although these will wear down naturally if a lot of concrete walking is done (roads and pavements), they still should be checked each time, some will still require to be trimmed. Dogs who are exercised on grass, fields or softer ground are likely to need theirs trimming every time. If they are left to grow they will eventually curl round and grow into their pads. Nail trimming is something most salons and vets offer. If you are not keen to cut their nails then let the professionals do it but don't just leave them – See Appendix 5 for how to cut nails.

Eyes – Many breeds have the problem of overflow of tears onto the face, which stains their fur in an array of orange and brown shades. This is very noticeable in white dogs and cats and those with the flat faces. There are many products on the market to prevent, reduce or remove the staining, personally I am unsure if any of these work. But here's the pro's guide to looking after their autumnal-coloured eyes:

> Wipe daily with a good quality eye cleaner, use separate cotton wool pieces for each eye.
>
> Be careful not to rub too hard, as you can end up removing the fur and making the skin sore.
>
> Dry thoroughly afterwards.
>
> Take them regularly to the groomers, who will cut the hair away from around the eyes.
>
> Their faces will start to smell if the eyes and surrounding skin are never cleaned.

Bath and blow dry

In many cases bathing your pet at home can turn into something that represents a bad form of aqua aerobics! This can be due to facilities available, the size of your pet and as well, pets are like children in that they will play their owners up something chronic but behave like butter wouldn't melt for someone else (even the pets are turning into Kevin and Perry!) So it can be easier to take them to the salon for their bath and dry.

Most salons will also have a range of shampoos and conditioners to suit your pet's skin and hair, there is no such thing as a 'one shampoo suits all', just like there is no such thing as 'one handbag suits all' occasions! Although you want to avoid too many baths (as this can create dry skin and hair) they can happily have a bath in-between their full grooms with no ill effects. Or every 6–8 weeks if they have short hair. You may want to bath and dry them at home (or try!) – see later on how to do this, there's a way to do this properly too!

Hand stripping

Certain breeds such as the Border terrier or other wire hair breeds, need their coats stripping or plucking approximately twice a year, which generally falls in line with the seasonal moults. These breeds have far more primary hairs giving the coat the wire, course-type texture. As it is the dead hair that is plucked out, it doesn't hurt – but there is a technique to it and it may hurt if this is done incorrectly. If you prefer to strip the coat yourself ask your groomer to show you how first. Under the tummy, the groin and armpit areas are generally not plucked as these are very sensitive, so may be trimmed instead. These breeds shouldn't be bathed or clipped as it alters the texture of the hair.

Other treatments to consider for our pets are, those that help shedding, massage, face trims, teeth brushing, dental care, weight checks, sunscreen application, flea and worm treatments, microchipping, to name a few. Very funky ideas such as nail painting, glitter, hair dye and gels are starting to sweep the country! As long as they are specific pet products no harm should be done, it's always wise to patch test first. Not all salons offer these treatments but ask what services your local salon offer, as they do vary.

Knots

Oh man, these are a nightmare! Knots begin as a small tangle which, if not combed out will develop in to a knot. If the knot isn't dealt with the coat will then start to develop into matts, turning your beloved pet into a walking piece of carpet (even if it does look like one from the Laura Ashley range, this is so not good). Underneath the knots, the skin starts to become sore, dry and painful, particularly on movement. Common areas when hair will knot are behind the ears, the armpit area and legs.

To help prevent knots forming, comb hair every few days from the root to the tip using a metal-toothed comb, the ones with rounded ends are best as they are less likely to scratch the skin (see image on p63). Don't rub the feet and legs dry with a towel after a walk, squeeze with the towel instead and ideally dry them with a hair dryer using a slicker brush (see image on p64). If you are struggling with their hair and knots, speak to your salon sooner rather than later.

Knots and matted coats cause groomers multiple headaches and cause distress to your pet. Skill and expertise are needed to remove these and they take a long time to get out. It is painful for your dog or cat – with the best will in the world there will always be a certain degree of tugging and pulling which hurts at the time and afterwards. The skin can be sensitive and sore, even red. Your dog or cat may behave strangely afterwards but should return to normal after a few days. If the knots or matts are large and too close to the skin, the only viable option will be to clip their hair off and start again. This too can leave your pet acting strangely e.g. unusually quiet, they may shiver as they will feel the cold more. Shivering is one of the ways the body can increase its own temperature. Wrap them up in their favourite blankets or use doggie jumpers to help keep them warm.

For cats, it is advisable not to let them out (particularly at night) until they have acclimatised to their new (non-existent) coat! Blankets, small jumpers, hooded beds can help keep them warm too.

Professional groomers (good ones) are worth their weight in gold, just like a good hairdresser is. There are some excellent groomers about and some dodgy ones (see Appendix 7 for what to ask and look for when finding a groomer).

Bathing your dog or cat at home

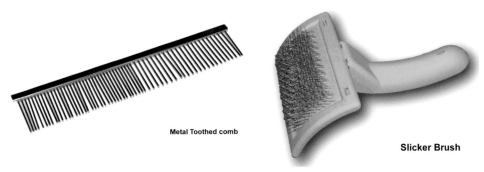

Metal Toothed comb

Slicker Brush

Before you choose this option (unless your pet is of the short-hair variety) then blow drying is needed after their bath (will you do this?). Not blow drying longer hair will encourage it to tangle and knot. **Do not use human or baby shampoo on pets**. Human skin may have a pH of 5.5 but pet's skin has a pH of 7.3. Therefore human or baby shampoos are too acidic for pet's skin. Dry, flaky skin can occur as a result as well as making them itch.

Some cats don't mind a wet bath and blow dry, but many do. In these cases a dry bath (dry shampoos) are a better option. Dry shampoos are also super for small dirty areas on dogs. A dry shampoo is liquid in a spray or foam format that's applied to the coat and rubbed in, the hair is then combed or brushed and voila! All done!

If plunging for the wet option, follow the steps below for salon-looking hair!

Adjust the water so it is <u>warm</u>.

Wet them, starting at the back legs and bottom and work forward to their head.

Be careful not to get water down their ears as this can lead to ear infections.

Ensure they are properly wet, otherwise your shampoo won't lather correctly – some breeds, due to their waterproof coats, take a few goes with the shower to ensure they are wet (Labradors and the Siberian Husky for example).

Apply your shampoo from the back end to the head. I doubt your pet will let you put one of those kiddie visor things on their heads, to stop shampoo and water going in their eyes, so you'll just have to be careful.

Rinse off the shampoo starting at the head and working backwards. Ensure all the shampoo is rinsed out, if not their hair will look greasy when it is dried.

Squeeze excess water out from their legs and towel-dry.

Dry them with a hair dryer; if they have a short coat, they can be left to dry naturally but keep the environment warm whilst they are drying off.

If you need to blow dry, use a low-heat setting and keep the drying moving – holding it one place for too long hurts and can cause burns.

Use slicker brushes (see Hair Image 3) to brush and dry at the same time, this will help prevent knots forming whilst drying and will aid getting any out that may be there already. Be gentle as the pins can make the skin red and sore. Cat's skin is more easily damaged than dog's, so extra care is needed with the puss cats.

Finishing sprays or deodorising sprays – these are used on dry hair and are great! They can be used as much or as little as you like, whenever you feel the need really! They work by eliminating the pet odour and replace it with gorgeousness! Don't get the 24-hour roll-on deodorant out though, it won't work and will leave white marks!

Now you're good to go, lights, camera, action!

Call 999!

OMG, there's blood everywhere, from a cut as wide as the Grand Canyon, 'he's never gonna make it!' Alright, alright chill, we are cool, unflappable geniuses and you can deal with this. Or at least you will after reading this chapter!

Your pet is very unlikely to go through life without injuring itself, eating something they shouldn't have or ending up in a situation that sends you into a blind panic. There are many types of first aid situations and they can happen anywhere – in the home, on a walk, on holiday or while looking after somebody else's pet. This chapter is about the common predicaments our pets might get in to, how or why they occur and what you can do until professional help is available.

If and when an accident or injury occurs, you are **not** going to run around screaming while trying to find your phone in your pocket or at the bottom of your bag. You **are,** going to remain calm, **consider your own safety first** and remember the aims of first aid:

1. Preserve life.

2. Alleviate pain and prevent further suffering.

3. Prevent the situation from deteriorating, ensuring no further damage is caused.

Interestingly, as the law stands, anyone who is involved in a road traffic accident where a dog is injured must report the incident to the police. The same law does not apply to cats or wildlife.

Foreign bodies and poisons

We will start with one of our trendy pet's favourite habits – eating. They don't realise that sometimes there are certain things they really shouldn't eat Why they feel the need to munch through a smelly sweaty sock that's been inside your son's football trainer for 1½ hours is beyond me? Eating certain objects can result in them becoming stuck, commonly this is either in the stomach or the intestines but objects can also become caught in the mouth, throat and oesophagus (food pipe) as well. They get stuck because the body cannot digest and break them down, they are too large to pass through or the object has pierced a bodily tissue and can't dislodge itself. We call 'things that get stuck' Foreign Bodies, here are some examples that I have seen removed over the years:

- Bits of plastic toys

- Balls

- Socks
- Nectarine stones
- Part of a corn on the cob
- Matching his and hers underwear, it wasn't from Rigby and Peller so not considered too much of a loss!
- Needles – this is common in cats as they like to play and chew the thread often attached, which can result in the needle being swallowed.
- Chicken bones and other types of bones
- Fish hooks

Contrary to popular belief, we do not have eyes in the back of our heads! So, how do you know if your pet has a foreign body if you haven't seen them eat it?

This is dependent on where it is stuck but common signs are: drooling, retching, difficulty or refusing to eat, vomiting, diarrhoea or constipation. If they do eat and drink they are unlikely to keep this down. Abdominal pain is very common and they may guard their tummies if you try to touch them. Remember an animal in pain can turn aggressive – we don't want one of your fingers in there as well!

If you can see something in their mouths the temptation is to pull it out with your hand, this can work but if you are unsure do not attempt it. Sharp objects, e.g. a fish hook, can damage and tear tissue when you pull, or you can push the object further back towards the throat, blocking their airway and their ability to breath.

If you suspect or know an object is stuck, collect any half-eaten objects that might be left and ring your vet. To confirm a foreign body your pet will usually have an X-ray or ultrasound scan to determine if there is one there and also its whereabouts. The end result is, more often than not, surgery to remove it.

The other problem with eating things they shouldn't is that they can be poisonous. The following list covers some of the more common ones but more information can be sourced from the BVA Animal Welfare Foundation or RSPCA (see useful contacts):

Chocolate

Medications such as Ibuprofen, Paracetamol

Rat/mice poisons

Slug/snail pellets (Metaldehyde)

Anti-freeze – this tastes really sweet and they love it

Batteries

Dishwasher powder

Caffeine – clean up spilt coffee granules

Conkers

Grapes/raisins/sultanas/currants

Lilies – especially for cats

Foxgloves

Mistletoe

Laburnum

Holly

Coal

Wax candles/crayons

Chalk

Oral contraceptives/hormone replacement therapy tablets

If they have being poisoned or you think they might have, first remove them from the source – they might not be very happy about this, particularly if they are half way through the Green & Blacks, but tough! Collect any evidence, wrappers, leaflets, packets, labels etc. and check the approximate time you think they have eaten their chosen poison. If they have been sick, note the contents and any colour – hold your nose if you have to but just do it!

Contact your vet immediately. Do not make them sick unless your vet tells you to do this, making them sick is the correct treatment for some poisons but not all – why? Some are irritant and corrosive and the damage caused when they first ingested them will be caused again when they bring the product back up. Inducing vomiting also needs to be done within a certain time frame of it being eaten.

If they have managed to cover themselves in something like tar, before taking them to the vets, preventing ingestion of the substance is key. Cats in particular will groom like crazy trying to get it off. Use an Elizabethan collar or place a child's vest/T-shirt over them until you get to the vets.

Hypothermia (too cold) and hyperthermia (too hot)

Hypothermia involves the body temperature dropping abnormally low. This may occur following exposure to cold temperatures for a prolonged period e.g. outside all night in freezing temperatures (should have wrapped up warm like mother said!), locked in outbuildings or they may have been immersed in cold water e.g. fallen in a lake and can't get out.

At this point you need to prevent further heat loss and warm the animal slowly. This can be done by:

- Drying the coat thoroughly using towels or a warm <u>not</u> hot hairdryer – this is not the time to be 'Nicky Clarke', just waft the dryer generally all over. Keep the dryer moving, holding it in one place for too long can cause burns to the skin.
- Wrap them in bubble wrap or space blankets or use normal blankets, coats, jumpers whatever you have available as an alternative.
- Warm <u>not</u> hot wheat pads or warm hot-water bottles.

Ring your vet and follow their advice, expect to have to take your pet to the practice.

Hyperthermia involves an excessive rise in body temperature. Typically this will happen following overheating e.g. being locked in car on a warm day, or they are unable to dissipate heat e.g. over-exercising on a warm day. Obese animals are more prone to hyperthermia as fat layers provide insulation, therefore preventing heat loss.

Either way these hotties need cooling down, try these techniques:

- Spraying (spray guns, shower, hosepipe) or immersing them in cool water – NOT COLD water as this constricts the blood vessels in the skin preventing heat loss.
- Cover with cool, wet towels.
- Set up a fan, this allows evaporation of heat and also helps to provide some well-needed fresh air for them.

Ring your vet and follow their advice, expect to have to take your pet to the practice.

Choking

The horror of the boiled sweet comes to mind here which managed to lodge itself at the back of my throat, a very scary moment! Similar can happen to pets, more so in dogs than cats and you do have to act quickly. They will have bulging eyes, paw at the face and try to cough. You can try and remove the item with your fingers or forceps but great care must be taken not to push the item further back. Suspending the pet by its hind legs is very helpful, letting the object fall forward and allowing some air to pass from the nose into the throat, the object could fall out completely. The other option is the Heimlich manoeuvre – See Appendix 8 for, 'How to perform the Heimlich manoeuvre'. The pressure applied, causes the animal to cough and forces obstruction forward and out of the mouth. This must not be performed more than four times as there is a risk of internal injuries. They can be distressed afterwards, so watch for them nipping or biting once the object has been removed. Ring your vet as they will need to examine them to check everything is OK internally.

Haemorrhaging (bleeding)

The site of blood often induces panic, please try and avoid this by remaining the person in control – how fab will you look if you deal with this situation effectively? Sometimes it can look worse than it is, this is particularly so where ear pinnas, pads and nails are concerned.

Bleeding comes in three forms and each looks different. It is important to understand the differences as this will denote the treatment and how urgent it is.

- Arterial bleeding – bleeding from an artery. This is the most serious and spectacular form of bleeding i.e. URGENT. It is bright red and spurts out of the wound in a pulse-type fashion, in rhythm with the heartbeat. The spurts of blood can go some distance so expect to get splatted!

- Venous bleeding – bleeding from a vein. This is less serious than arterial bleeding, the blood appears a darker red colour and the loss is slower (it rarely pulsates out).

- Capillary bleeding – bleeding from capillaries (small blood vessels). This is rarely dangerous, the blood tends to ooze from numerous pinpoint sites of the wound, a bit like a graze.

Controlling the red stuff

Whatever the type or wherever it is coming from, bleeding has to be stopped or at least controlled until you get to the vets. Mental note – if the wound has something stuck in it, like half a stick or a large piece of glass, do not, I repeat, do not remove it. Leave it in there as it is acting as its own blood clotting device, take it out and the bleeding will increase tenfold. Apply your chosen method of control around it.

- Digital pressure – pressure is applied directly to the site using clean fingers or clean material (not tissues). If the blood seeps through the material just add more on top, do not remove to replace with a new piece. This closes the bleeding vessel and prevents further loss. Fast, easy and effective, you will need to apply the pressure for five minutes to ensure enough time for a clot to form.

- Pressure pads or bandages – absorbent padding is applied to the wound and bandaged in place. Again if blood seeps through do not remove but add further layers on top. See Appendix 4 for 'How to bandage a foot' and follow the steps to make it a pressure bandage. This is a better method to use for wounds that require control for longer than digital pressure. As these bandages are tighter do not leave on for more than fifteen minutes as tissue damage can occur.

- Tourniquets – a tourniquet is a long piece of bandage or material. In an emergency, items such as a shoe lace, scarf or tie can be used. The bandage or material is tied tightly above the bleeding wound. This occludes the bleeding blood vessel and stops the bleeding. Due to the nature of this do not leave on for more than ten minutes, as tissue and nerve damage can occur. Tourniquets can only be used on lower legs and tails and in all honesty I would only apply these on the advice of a vet or vet nurse.

Cut pads

This can happen so easily and is very common. They might have slipped on a dodgy rock or stone (they're not wearing heels though so what's their excuse?), they could have stood on a piece of glass or the pad may have being cut accidently with scissors, if you were trying to remove hair or knots from the feet for example. For most small to medium sized cuts the following should suffice until you speak to your vet. You may need two people to do this:

- If possible, flush the cut with saline or water. This is to remove any dirt and debris from the cut.

- Stop and prevent further bleeding, usually digital pressure followed by a bandage is fine.

- Cover the wound – see Appendix 4 on 'How to Bandage a foot'. If bandaging equipment is not available, stop or control any bleeding and cover with a sock, glove or small plastic bag and tape on.

For larger wounds a pressure bandage may be needed. Don't forget to get someone to time how long the bandage is on for. Ring your vet who will probably want to see your pet; antibiotics and pain relief may well be needed.

Bleeding or ripped nails

Don't you just hate it when that happens! Catching their nails is a common thing particularly with dew claws which is why they are so often removed as puppies (in the domestic dog, dew claws don't really serve a purpose). If they have caught the nail quite badly, it may look like it is hanging off or may come off completely. This exposes the nail bed which looks like a pink/red stumpy bit and is actually really painful (think about if you ripped the entire nail off one of your fingers or toes – OK don't think about it!). You need to ring your vets who will probably want to see your pet. You can flush the nail area with saline or water to wash away dirt and apply a paw bandage (see Appendix 4 'How to Bandage') if they will let you – remember this is uncomfortable and you are likely to need two people. The bandage will act as protection and comfort. If the bandage idea isn't happening, tape on a large cotton sock – no fluffy pink socks or cashmere ones please as 'bits' can stick onto the sore nail. Prevent them from licking or chewing it – see Appendix 3 'How to prevent self-interference'. Your pet may well need antibiotics to prevent infection and some sort of pain relief. Your vet may need to remove the rest of the nail if it has only partially come off. Either way they recover well from this and the nail does grow back!

Seizures, fits or convulsions

These result from a disruption of electrical activity in the brain and can have various causes which are beyond the scope of this chapter. These can look quite frightening but don't be frightened, get a grip and help your pet; he's banking on you at this point.

A few minutes before a fit starts they are often restless or excitable. During the actual fit, they usually lose consciousness and paddle with their legs whilst lying on their sides. Jerky movements also occur and they may well empty their bladder and/or bowels. This part can last a few minutes. Afterwards they are disorientated and restless which usually lasts around a few hours. There are different types of fits, not all of them result in loss of consciousness and the jerky movements, they can just stand and stare or have slight twitching. While they are having the fit, move any objects out of the way that may cause an injury. You can move the pet to an area of safety but beware they can bite during a fit. Dim or turn off any lights, turn all radios, music and televisions off and keep noise to an absolute minimum. If your pet does not come out of the fit, this is an emergency and you need to see your vet immediately.

If your pet suffers from fits on a regular basis, then you are probably familiar with this and have your own routine and medication. If however this is the first time your pet has had a fit, phone your vet for them to examine them.

Burns

The most common type of burns are thermal burns. These are burns caused by either:

- Dry heat such as a fire, cooker hob, heat pads, or more likely in our case, hairdryers and hair straighteners!
- Scalds caused by heated liquids including water and oils.

Burns need to be seen by a vet, but you can help by flushing the area with saline or water to rinse off any dirt or debris – a slow rinse of water (though don't try and power hose it). Cooling the burn down is the main priority which can be done by immersing the injured part in cold water, applying ice packs or wrapping in a cold wet towel. Take care with this – your pet will not like it, as it will hurt. Surface burns are actually far more painful than very deep severe burns. Cover the burn with cling film to help prevent fluid loss and dehydration and take to the vets immediately.

Burns can also occur from:

- Electricity – e.g. chewing through wires. With any type of electrical burn, TURN THE POWER OFF FIRST before touching them or anything else. **Do not forget to do this**.
- Chemicals – bleach for example, keep products like these out of reach.
- Cold injury – prolonged contact with ice.
- Radiation – can occur following radiation therapy.

Insect stings

Wasps and bees are the main culprits here and obviously these are more common in the summer months (or the months where it is meant to be summer seeing as we are in the UK!). Pets seem to love to chase and play with these which often mean stings on their faces and paws. Pain and swelling occur but this usually settles down. It is the poison from the sting that causes the pain not the bee or wasp penetrating the skin. If the bee's sting is still in the skin, try and not remove it using tweezers. This can squash it, causing more of the poison to be released. Try removing by scraping something like a credit card or your nail.

Bee stings are acidic and you can treat the sting by applying an alkaline solution of bicarbonate of soda. (Remember bicarb for bee, B to B.)

Wasp stings are alkaline and you can treat the sting by applying an acidic solution like vinegar. (I remember this as VW, like the car except it stands for vinegar wasp!)

These stings are usually not dangerous, unless they are stung around the throat or neck area and the swelling interferes with their breathing. Multiple stings from an angry mob of bees or wasps can cause a dangerous reaction, a single wasp if irritated enough can sting several times. In these cases ring your vet immediately and follow the advice.

Vomiting and Diarrhoea

The dreaded vomiting and diarrhoea can occur from simple things such as eating too much, scavenging, to more serious problems like Parvo virus. If either of these continues for more than 24–48 hours, contains blood or they are a young puppy and kitten, then you must see your vet.

In the first instance, your pet needs starving for 24 hours, they will make you feel guilty for this one but don't give in – you're the responsible one here!

Access to water must always be available.

After this time, (and much cleaning up!) food can be reintroduced slowly. The type of food offered is important. It needs to be bland and highly digestible so not to irritate the stomach and intestines any further e.g. use food such as chicken, turkey, white fish, see the protein part in 'For the main course I would like…' for more information on this. The following day, small amounts of food can be offered 3–4 times a day, the whole amount fed should equal no more than half their normal daily amount.

The next day continue with the same, increasing the total amount to no more than three quarters of their normal daily amount.

If all is still well, on the third day, they can be fed their normal amount but still using the bland food.

After this you can start to introduce their normal diet over a period of seven days. Mix their normal food in with the bland food in small amounts, slowly increase their normal food while decreasing the bland one, until normality has returned!

If at any point they start to vomit or pass diarrhoea again, return to the previous day's guide. If nothing is improving and they are deteriorating you need to phone your vet.

Paraphimiosis (protruding swollen penis)

The erect penis can become too engorged with blood, leaving it unable to return into the prepuce. It looks very swollen with the end of the prepuce appearing to 'cut into' the swollen penis. After a while the tissues start to dry out making it more difficult to return it back into the prepuce. It can become incredibly painful as it remains protruded. It can happen to the best of them, no giggles or "I am not doing that". We shall be grown up and… Just get on with it!

Apply ice packs to the swollen penis to help reduce the blood flow, pinching the skin just in front of the scrotum will also help reduce the size of the engorged penis.

If the tissues have become dry (which is likely) apply KY jelly or liquid paraffin to the area.

Phone your vet and let them take it from here. The majority of the time they will be able to return it to its normal place, in some cases surgery is need to enlarge the prepuce opening.

There, all done. You can forget about it now, you dog will be much happier too!

First aid kit

A good plan is to have a basic first aid kit for your pet in your home or car (never mind about ours!). This way you will have to hand the necessary to cover the basics like a cut pad or bleeding ear, plus you look all organised and clever!

Use a sensible hard container and fill with:

- Sterile saline solution
- Gauze pads
- Vaseline impregnated wound dressing
- Cotton wool
- Bandages
- Micropore tape or similar
- Outer protective wraps for bandages
- Extra swabs or cloths – for use with digital pressure to help stem bleeding.
- A pre-cut long length piece of bandage which can be used as a muzzle if needed or tourniquet.
- Scissors
- Gloves – the latex kind not leather!
- Cling film
- Space blanket or bubble wrap
- Your vet's phone number and other relevant emergency contact details.
- Pen and paper to write down any instructions.
- No flashing blue lights or sirens to put on your car – sorry!

Appendix 1

How to brush your pet's teeth

1. Start by having everything ready and to hand. Push the toothpaste or gel into the bristles of the toothbrush, otherwise you tend to find it falls off or is flicked everywhere but where you want.

2. Approach from the side, hold the muzzle with one hand using the thumb to lift the jowl out of the way.

3. Slide the toothbrush in and begin brushing in a circular motion ensuring all teeth and the gum line are brushed.

4. Repeat step 3 for the other side.

5. Brush the incisors last, these can tickle and quite often pets will react to these being brushed, hence it's better to leave these till the end so you have more chance of brushing the rest. Approach from the front using one hand to hold the muzzle and using the thumb to lift it up the lip, again brush in circular motions over the teeth and gum line.

You do not have to open your pet's mouth as if they need to say aahh and you don't have to worry about brushing the insides of the teeth. The saliva coupled with the tongue action is enough to keep the insides of the teeth relatively clean.

Appendix 2
How to change your pet on to a new food

Changing your pet's food suddenly can cause them tummy upsets. They can often vomit, have diarrhoea or even just a tummy ache. The best way to avoid this is following the below guidelines:

1. Mix a small amount of the new diet in with their current diet, keep to this ratio for a couple of days.

2. After this time, increase the amount of the new diet while decreasing the current diet.

3. Continue in this manner until the new diet has completely replaced their old one. Ideally this should be done over a period of approximately a week.

4. If they are not enjoying their new dinner, try adding <u>small amounts of one,</u> of these tempting 'dips'!

   Gravy.

   Fry it in a small amount of butter.

   Sardines or pilchards in tomato sauce (cats absolutely adore this).

   Add water to dry food.

   Pieces of chicken, ham, beef.

   Wet cat food (dogs absolutely adore this).

   Warm the food.

Appendix 3

How to prevent self-interference
(itching, rubbing, chewing and pulling)

Please discuss with your vet or vet nurse which one of these or combination of these is the most suitable for your pet:

1. Use distraction, offer treats or play to keep them occupied.

2. Cover their feet with either socks, (which can be taped on) or use doggie boots/socks – available at most vets or pet shops. This prevents them using their nails to itch and prevents them interfering with any wound/sore on the feet or lower leg.

3. Bandage the affected area.

4. If the sore or itchy area is on the tummy or on the back, you can use T-shirts (pet or children's ones are fine). Baby vest can be used for small dogs and cats, this keeps the area covered so they can't get to it or rub it on furniture etc.

5. Elizabethan collars (Buster collars, lampshades, buckets, funnels, call them what you will!).These can be useful; it prevents them from being able to get to their ears or any other area on the head or face. It also prevents them from licking and chewing at other areas. You many find you need to remove the collar whilst they are eating and drinking and some prefer the clear versions rather than the opaque ones because they provide better visibility. Quite often pets dislike these as they 'feel funny' and because they prevent them from doing what they want to – but you have to weigh up which is better for them?

6. Neck braces can be used to prevent your pet from being able to get to certain areas e.g. back end, as they can't turn their head to get to them. These are a bit like a round squashy cushion and are much softer than Elizabethan collars and do not interfere with vision.

WARNING – Do not go near Elizabethan collars whilst your pet is wearing it if, you are wearing anything less than 80 denier tights or worse still, bare-legged. They do ladder tights, mark your legs and it flipping hurts!

Appendix 4

Applying a limb bandage

It is generally easier if two people do this; have everything laid out within reach before you start.

With limb bandages you need to include the foot to stop any swelling (unless you are applying a special type of bandage called a Robert Jones, these are used for broken limbs or after surgery to the bones or knee joint but let's master this one first!).

A bandage applied to the limb needs to include a joint above and below within the bandage – helps to prevent swelling and to keep it on!

Place cotton wool in between the toes and pads (not rolled up bits of cotton wool as this is uncomfortable). The cotton wool is there to stop rubbing and to absorb any sweat.

Place of a piece of wound dressing over the cut (if present) e.g. Melolin.

Place cotton wool around the limb including the paw.

Next is the bandage: start at the front of the foot, roll it underneath the foot and behind, only to the carpus (wrist) or tarsus (hock). Hold this bit with a spare finger from your other hand. Loop the bandage back on itself and roll the bandage back underneath to the front, again catch this with one of your fingers (don't let go of the back piece!). Repeat this, then twist the bandage and start to wrap it around the limb.

Cover two thirds of the previous layer, applying slight tension (by pulling it). Ensure the foot and the correct part of the limb are covered evenly. Bumpy bandages create uneven pressure, are uncomfortable and can create sores. Cut the bandage and stick using tape, or tie in a small bow.

Apply the outer protective wrap in the same way. These are self-conforming (stick to themselves), meaning you need to pull the length out first before wrapping it round.

Rolling it round like a bandage will tighten it far too much. Once it is all covered, cut the wrap and smooth down (as it will stick to itself).

Pressure bandages

These are applied in the same way except the tension applied when rolling the bandage round is far greater i.e. pulls it more. The outer protective wrap may on this occasion be rolled to create further pressure. Remember only leave this on for 10 minutes.

Practice on your teddies or your other half (if they will let you play doctors and nurses). This way you know what to do should the need arise.

How to apply a bandage

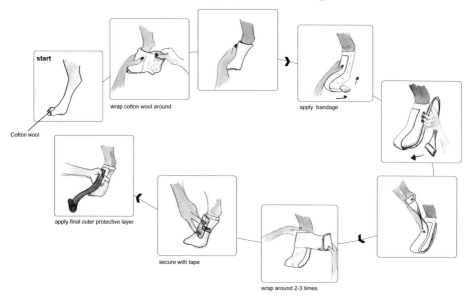

start

Cotton wool

wrap cotton wool around

apply bandage

wrap around 2-3 times

secure with tape

apply final outer protective layer

Appendix 5

How to cut nails

Short nails have a
short blood vessel

WRONG

cut here

This shows the correct
way to clip the nail.

Appendix 6

How to clean ears

1. Hold the ear flap up or hold the tip in the case of upright ears and place the tip of the ear cleaner into the ear canal.

2. Apply 1 or 2 drops into the canal (be ready, as they are likely to shake their head, particularly if too much has been applied).

3. Massage the base of the ear to allow the cleaner to fully circulate around the canal, picking up dirt on the way.

4. Using cotton wool wipe around the ear. This will remove any excess cleaner, dirt and wax. Do not use cotton buds down the ear canal.

Clean the ears once or twice a week. This method can also be used for applying antibiotic drops into the ear except you would miss out step number 4.

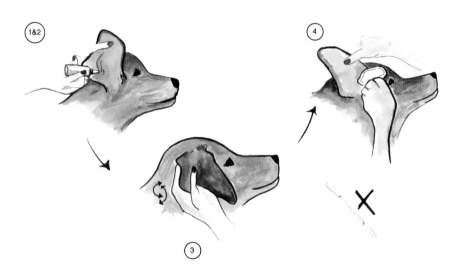

Appendix 7

How to choose a pet groomer

As with any industry there is good and bad, and pet grooming is certainly no different. Here are some tips on what to look for and ask when searching for a good pet groomer:

1. Ask your friends and family who they use. If you see a pet that looks good ask the owner where they go. Personal recommendation is also best.

2. Legally a qualification does not have to be gained in order to operate as a pet groomer. Ask the groomer how long they have being grooming and the type of work they have experience with. You can also ask to see their certificate of qualification, often these are on display. Any groomer worth their salt will not be offended by asking these sorts of questions.

3. Do they work on an appointment system or do they keep your pet for half a day/all day? From your pet's point of view an appointment slot is better than being somewhere all day.

4. Go and see the salon. A good salon should be clean, tidy and not smell. Where are the pets housed? Are they safe? Do they have access to water and comfortable bedding whilst they are not being groomed?

5. If cats are being groomed as well, the groomer should have experience in handling cats as these are very different creatures to dogs and have very different requirements. Cats must be groomed and housed separately to dogs. Dogs are seen as the predator and will make the cat feel unsecure and stressed, in turn causing all sorts of problems. Dogs and cats facing each other in a kennel situation is an absolute no no.

6. Meet the groomer. They should be happy to discuss your pet, your requirements and any concerns or questions. Do you like them? The groomer should know the standard breed cut but should also be asking and listening to what you want. If you don't know, they should be able to talk through different options with you. A good groomer will be able to scissor trim as well as be able to do clipping/shaving work.

7. A good groomer will always meet you at EVERY appointment and discuss your requirements EACH time.

8. The following should ALWAYS be standard within a full grooming appointment: Ears cleaned and plucked, eyes cleaned, nails trimmed, anal glands expressed.

9. Ask how bad behaviour is dealt with. The use of muzzles and a second person for restraint and distraction are perfectly acceptable ways. Hitting, shouting, rough handling or plaguing them is not.

10. Honesty. There are hundreds of breeds and it is unlikely that even the best of groomers will have experience in all of them. However a good groomer will be honest if they have not groomed a particular breed before and will research the breed before undertaking it. If the groomer is honest about things like this or if your pet has not behaved the best that day you can be assured they are telling the truth when they have behaved well or they know the said cuts, styles and breeds.

11. A groomer should always give advice on how best to look after your pet's coat at home, e.g. how to prevent knots, which type of comb or brush to use.

Appendix 8

The Heimlich Manoeuvre

In small dogs and cats

Ideally use two people.

Suspend the animal by its hind legs.

Apply a sharp thrust just below the rib cage in a downward movement.

You may repeat this four times.

In large dogs

If the dog is too large to be suspended by its hind legs:

Lay the dog on its side, although this can be performed in the standing position as well.

Raise the hind quarters as high as you can with the head lower than the rest of the body.

Clench your hands together around their abdomen just below the rib cage and apply a sharp thrust in an upward movement.

You may repeat this four times.

Remember they may well bite or attempt to bite after the object has being removed.

Place hands under ribs

Useful Contacts

Association of Pet Dog Trainers (APDT)
PO Box 17
Kempsford
GL7 4WZ
Tel. 01285 810811
www.apdt.co.uk

Bayer
Animal Health Division
Bayer House
Strawberry Hill
Newbury
RG14 1JA
www.bayer.co.uk

British Veterinary Nursing Association (BVNA)
82 Greenway Business Centre
Harlow Business Park
Harlow
Essex
CM19 5QE
Tel. 01279 408644
Fax. 01279 408645
www.bvna.org.uk

British Veterinary Association
7 Mansfield Street
London
W1G 9NQ
Tel. 020 7636 6451
Fax. 020 7908 6349
www.bva.co.uk

Cats Protection
National Cat Centre
Chelwood Gate
Haywoods Heath
Sussex
RH17 7TT
National Helpline: 0300012 12 1 2
www.cats.org.uk

CEVA Animal Health
www.ceva.com

Department for Environment Food and Rural Affairs (DEFRA)
Nobel House
17 Smith Square
London
SW1P 3JR
Helpline 08459 33 55 77
www.defra.gov.uk

Dogs Trust
17 Wakely Street
London
EC1V 7RQ
Tel. 0207 837 0006
www.dogstrust.org.uk

European Scientific Counsel Companion Animal Parasites (ESCCAP)
www.esccap.org

Eukanuba
www.eukanuba.co.uk

Feline Advisory Bureau (FAB)
Taeselbury
High Street
Tisbury
Wiltshire

SP3 6LD
Tel. 01747 871872
Fax. 01747 871873
www.fabcats.org

Hill's pet Nutrition Ltd
Building 5
Croxley Green Business Park
Watford
WD18 8YL
Tel. 0800 282438
ww.hillspet.co.uk

Iams
Tel. 0808 100 70 10
www.iams.co.uk

James Wellbeloved
Crown Pet Foods Ltd
Oak Tree Meadow
Blackworthy Road
Castle Cary
Somerset
BA7 7PH
Tel. 0845 603 9095
Fax. 0845 300 6320
www.wellbeloved.com

Jez Rose
Canine and Wolf Behaviour Specialist
Tel. 0800 8600 156
www.jezrose.co.uk

The Kennel Club
1–5 Clarges Street
Piccadilly
London
W1J 8AB
Tel. 0844 463 3980
Fax. 020 7518 1028
www.thekennelclub.org.uk
Lily's Kitchen (Organic pet food)
PO Box 59287
Vale of Heath

London
NW3 9JR
Tel. 0207 433 1863
www.lilyskitchen.co.uk

Merial Animal Health
CM19 5TG
Tel. 01279 775858
www.merial.com

National Missing Pets Register
16 Richmond Avenue
Thornton-Cleveleys
Lanacashire
FY5 2BP
www.nationalpetregister.org

National Pet Sitters
PO Box 1433
Oxford
OX4 9AU
Tel. 0845 2308544
www.dogsit.com

Nina Ottosson interactive dog toys and games
www.interactivedoggames.com

Pet Care Trust
Bedford Business Centre
170 Mile Road
Bedford
MK42 9TW
Tel. 01234 273933
Fax. 01234 273550
www.petcare.org.uk

Pets Kitchen
(Natural and hypoallergenic pet food, developed by TV vet Joe Inglis)
Unit 17 Horcott Industrial Estate
Horcott Road
Fairfood
Gloucestershire
GL7 4BX
Tel. 0845 303 8643
www.petskitchen.co.uk

Petplan
Great West House (GW2)
Great West Road
Brentford
Middlesex
TW8 9DX
Tel. 0845 077 1934
www.petplan.co.uk

Professional Association of Applied Canine Trainers
0845 329668
www.paact.co.uk

Royal Canin
Crown Pet Foods Ltd
Oak Tree Meadow
Blackworthy Road
Castle Cary
Somerset
BA7 7PH
Tel. 0845 3005011
www.royalcanin.co.uk

Royal College of Veterinary Surgeons (RCVS)
Belgravia House
62–64 Horseferry Road
London
SW1P 2AF
Tel. 020 7222 2001
Fax. 020 7222 2004
www.rcvs.org.uk

RSPCA
Wilberforce Way
Southwater
Horsham
West Sussex
RH13 9RS
Cruelty line: 0300 1234 999
Advice line: 0300 1234 555
Donation line: 0300 123 0346
Fax. 0303 123 0100
www.rspca.org.uk

Sound Therapy 4 pets (Sounds Scary CD range and training help)
www.soundtherapy4pets.com

Virbac Animal Health UK
Woolpit Business Park
Windmill Avenue
Woolpit
Bury St Edmunds
Suffolk
IP31 9UP
Tel. 01359 243243
Fax. 01359 243200
www.virbac.co.uk

A very fab national campaign to promote responsible dog ownership.
www.nationaldogcampaign.co.uk

Contact the Author

Annaliese Morgan DipAVN (Surgical) RVN MBVNA
Fuchsia
15 Bradford Road
Brighouse
HD6 1RW
Tel 01484 714872
Email: info@fuchsiapetsonline.co.uk
www.fuchsiapetsonline.co.uk
www.twitter.com/fuchsiaonline

Illustrator:

Kate Crowther
www.watercoloursbykate.com
Email info@watercoloursbykate.com
Tel: 01422 382817